Fire the Imagination
WRITE ON!

Also by Dorit Winter

Because of Yolande
The Art and Science of Teaching Composition
Sheets of White Light
Train a Dog, but Raise the Child

Fire the Imagination
WRITE ON!

by
Dorit Winter

Waldorf
PUBLICATIONS
RESEARCH INSTITUTE FOR Waldorf EDUCATION

Printed with support from the Waldorf Curriculum Fund

Published by
Waldorf Publications at the
Research Institute for Waldorf Education
38 Main Street
Chatham, NY 12037

Title: *Fire the Imagination: Write On!*
Author: Dorit Winter
Cover art: Dorit Winter
Cover art photo: Afshin Jalalian
© 2017 by Waldorf Publications

ISBN 978-1-943582-05-1

Curriculum Series
The Publications Committee of the Research Institute is pleased to bring forward this publication as part of its Curriculum Series. The thoughts and ideas represented herein are solely those of the author and do not necessarily represent any implied criteria set by Waldorf Publications. It is our intention to stimulate as much writing and thinking as possible about our curriculum, including diverse views. Please contact us at patrice@waldorf-research.org with feedback on this publication as well as requests for future work.

Table of Contents

Preface

Literature and writing have always been my thing. I wrote my first story as an 8th grader at Junior High School 190 in Queens. In high school, inspired by Mrs. Christy Barnes, my English teacher at the Rudolf Steiner High School in New York City, I discovered poetry and great books. I received an MA in comparative literature. I've published books and articles. Manuscripts of two novels lie neglected in a drawer. Most importantly, there have been over four decades of teaching children and adults creative writing.

"Centivo" was the name of that 8th grade story. Centivo was a penny, and in exalted language, I enumerated his adventures. I still have that piece of juvenilia, and the self-aware tone of smug sophistication it exudes is awful. But more than half a century later, what I notice even more than the pseudo-writing is the very real theme. What fascinated me back then was the biography of the penny. I provided Centivo with a destiny. The story was my pre-adolescent take on karma. More than half a century later, that's a theme I'm still unraveling.

More than half a century later, 7th and 8th graders still express the tender, hidden, prescient depths of the pre-adolescent soul. Student writing, no matter the student's age, tends to be revelatory.

This book provides various exercises intended to enable the teacher of budding writers to focus on the building blocks of writing: word, sentence, paragraph. Precise instructions provide a firm foundation for writers of any age, but especially for hamstrung, inarticulate, I-can't-write writers. Adults, teenagers, and pre-adolescents have all surprised themselves with the relevance, the depth, the quality of the self-expression they achieve by following a few instructions.

The more precise the instructions, the more carefully engineered the writing's structure, the more objective the expectations, the more personal the story that will flow, dribble, or spatter onto the page. Although our goal is to elicit strongly crafted sentences, secrets of the soul will bloom on the page. Hidden truths will emerge. But only if we provide the right scaffold.

Children and youths take to the precise instructions of these exercises like ducks to water. Adults like them too, because they are eminently doable. As with exercises of any kind, practicing them results in fluency. These exercises show us what to look for in our students' writing and how to help them make it crisp, to make it sparkle, to make it interesting. Very rarely have I asked writing students to tell me how they *feel* about something. The emphasis is on observation, on word choice, on the telling detail. The result is clarity of sight, egress of insight, revelation of self.

The sequence of our attempts is logical. We start with individual words. By the end of our block, we have written several stories.

Huge walls of rock rise up from the edge of the pond.
They turn pink as they catch the light of the dying sun.
The emerald of the pond wilts into a deep black. Across
the water, evergreens extend to the glowing clouds as the
flaming sun descends behind them.

This is the beginning of a story about two boys on a camping trip by an 8th grade girl who told me she was "more interested in science than in writing."

I call this sort of description *pictorial writing*. There's room for improvement; there almost always is. This example leans a bit heavily on colors, which is okay, although pink, emerald, black and green are perhaps too much of a good thing. Still, the writer sees the picture she is creating. She experiences the picture. She comes up with "wilts" which is inventive and apt. The scene works. Not only does each sentence paint a picture the reader can see in his or her mind, the inherent transitions weave the sentences into an integrated whole. It's a picture, not a puzzle. It's reader-friendly and allows the reader easy access. It's a realistic, yet imagined scene. It portrays a world in which trees reach upward. It's not a world where anything goes; it's not a Harry Potter world. Imagined veracity is our turf.

The writer—child or adult—finds both artistic and scientific satisfaction in solving the problem of how to lasso the imagination through words. If there are too many adjectives, florid, indulged, noun-quenching sentences will be weighted by murky, confusing modifiers. If we use the same word too often, we'll sound stilted. If the cadence of our words never varies, we'll put the reader to sleep. But if we can train the imagination to adhere to the logic of the real world while creating a fictive reality, we'll find the most precise words to evoke an alternate reality that is true. "The highest exercise of imagination is not to devise what has no existence, but rather to perceive what really exists." Henry Wadsworth Longfellow nailed it precisely.

This is the imagination that elevates the writer's own soul, even as it captivates the reader. The least interested children, the least confident writers find themselves lured by the task. Our detailed instructions offer them security and build confidence. A measured training regime of exercises builds that confidence—and is fun.

Writing, especially creative writing, can be arduous and downright overwhelming for students of all ages. They feel incompetent and vulnerable. If we take the ingredients which make for good writing one at a time and work on them in such a way that they become fun rather than fearsome, the writers-in-training start the trajectory toward confident competence. It's important to tell the students at the outset of our campaign that each of them will have written several short stories by the end of the main lesson block or track class. We'll also be *reading* short stories.

I have taught dozens of 7th and 8th grade main lessons using variations on the following exercises. I have also used the same method to help adults become more articulate, more logical, more precise, and more coherent. This book is intended to help teachers of children, but it will reference the adult experience as well.

Note: Some Waldorf schools have an 8th grade "Creative Writing" main lesson, whereas others call it "Short Story." For our purposes here, these are one and the same: Whether the title emphasizes the one or the other, we write and read short stories in both. We write A LOT in both. We find we have things to say.

Becoming Word-Conscious

Most of us use language pragmatically, not artistically. We have something in mind, and we express it as directly as possible. Unless we are polyglots or poets, and are used to culling our words for their different flavors and the nuance we're after, we tend to spill our words into the air and onto the paper without much deliberation. Children, being the gifted mimics they are, will imitate the style of the adults around them. If the adult is deliberate and conscious and searches for the right word, the child will realize that there is choice in language. Learning to talk is a divine activity, a cosmic achievement.[1] The language enveloping the infant as he or she learns to talk, has far-reaching consequences.[2] By 7th or 8th grade and beyond, our work with creative writing re-enlivens the use of language.

So let's start with the essential building block of language: the word. Instead of settling for the first word that comes to mind, let's see how we can develop a sense for word choice. Let's see how we can become word-conscious.[3]

Generic – Specific

To create a picture in the mind of the reader, use the most specific word. This is especially true for nouns. Here is a sentence using generic words:

People went to the place.

You can ask the children to write down what they see in their mind's eye when they hear this sentence.

It'll become evident that this is a vague sentence. It's what I call a generic sentence. Everyone has a different idea of what it is meant to convey. Can we narrow the three main parts of the sentence to become more specific? How about:

Athletes ran on to the field.

Better, but can we get even more specific? What type of athletes? Soccer players? Hurdlers? Field hockey players? And where are these soccer players, these long distance runners? In a stadium? In a dusty, overgrown field? How can we make it more specific:

Hockey players jogged into the stadium.
Riders cantered into the ring.
Swimmers stepped onto their starting blocks.

These specific sentences are demonstrably more inviting than their more generic progenitor. As readers, we are immediately drawn into the picture they form in our mind.

There is nothing wrong with our original sentence, "People went to the place." It's just not a very descriptive sentence. It doesn't interest us as much as our more detailed, more specific, more pictorial examples.

1   *Rule Number One:*
     Use detailed, specific-word vocabulary.

To clarify the difference between the first generic sentence and the more specific offspring, we need to understand the difference between a *generic* noun and a *specific* noun. Although obvious for some students, this is a challenging concept for others, and because it is our foundation, we want to spend some time on it. I prefer to begin our course of study by focusing on the individual word in the complete sentence, because if we begin with the word alone, the enterprise is abstract. A sentence immediately has content which draws us in more than a word by itself. Of course, you can start with the word alone, too, and then build up the specific sentence.

To clarify the meaning of generic and specific, let's take some generic words, and see what we get as we become more specific. Provide the students with the first word, then ask them to come up with their own, more specific, variations. It will become quickly apparent that the name of the mountain or river or even the painting is the most specific, but to avoid this easy fix, I don't allow names, such as Mt. Kilimanjaro. I explain that this is in fact a wonderfully specific mountain, but it just doesn't work for this exercise which we are doing to become conscious of word choices.

Let's start with some given examples. Can we find some subsets, i.e., specific words? Let's do some conversions on the board together (*subset* and *conversion* are labels I've invented. I've found that by providing such labels, we convey a measure of scientific elevation to our task):

mountain – peak, ridge, bluff, mesa
tool – hammer, screwdriver, rake, scalpel
flower – marigold, honeysuckle, rose

Once you feel the students get the idea, give them the generic word, and see how many conversions we can come up with:

house – cottage, hut, mansion, castle
painting – drawing, sketch, pastel, cartoon, watercolor
plate – platter, saucer, bowl, dish
river – brook, cascade, creek, rivulet

We can also consider the qualities of the object, and come up with a sequence which is almost a story in itself.

food < meat – beef – tenderloin – medium rare – salty
fruit – apple – Pink Lady – sweet – grated – cooked
book – novel – biographical – historical – 19th century –
    Random House
furniture – bedroom – bed – bunk – wood – oak – painted –
    red – peeling
flower – poppy – California Poppy – blooming – yellow – faded

It's important at this early stage, that we agree on our choices. If a student argues that a particular word does not fit properly into the category of the generic word, for example, that "bowl" is not really a "plate," I consider the matter, and if I think there is some wiggle room, meaning, if it's not an obvious matter, I put parentheses around the suggested word. That usually takes care of it. If there is a word which really makes no sense in the lineup, I have to be sure, for the sake of the logical thinkers in the group, to erase it. Above all, logic has to hold sway. After all, we're after precision. Adults usually have a harder time with this than youngsters.

Holding up a visual dictionary works wonders at this stage. Most youngsters have never seen one. It's useful to have such a reference in the classroom. It provides the names for the parts of things, and also provides lots of comparable objects. We might look up *hat*, for example, and discover that we have a choice: beret, cloche, toque, southwester, panama, shapka, derby, boater, cap; not to mention examples which use a modifying adjective: cartwheel hat, knit cap, stocking cap, gob hat, pillbox hat, top hat, hunting cap, skullcap, garrison cap…. Who knew there were that many hats? The only problem with the visual dictionary is that you can get lost in it.

Another very useful source for synonyms is the *Oxford American Writer's Thesaurus*. It provides precise definitions, a slew of synonyms with explanations of their differences, and a host of examples, while also warning us of easy mixups.[4] I like to keep these reference books in the classroom. Later, we'll add *Home Ground*,[5] a treasury of terms denoting geographical features.

Having clarified the concept by working with words alone, let's now move to the sentence.

From Word to Sentence

Taking into account what we learned about word specificity, how can we improve this sentence?

Animals help human beings.

Let's look at the word *animal* and see how we can make it more specific, step by step:

animal – mammal – dog – retriever – Labrador Retriever

Once we know that our sentence starts with "Labrador Retriever," we can quickly improve on the rest of the sentence.

Labrador Retrievers guide blind pedestrians through busy streets.

We might transform *animal* in a completely different way:

animal – fish – salmon – Coho salmon

Is this too far from the original?

I love fishing for Coho salmon in Idaho.

A conversation about the content of the sentence, about the actual meaning of the words, will take the exercise out of a purely intellectual and abstract pursuit into a living reality. Perhaps fishing for the Coho in Idaho does help human beings. What kind of help would this be? Less obvious than the Labrador guiding the blind pedestrian, but who's to say it isn't truly therapeutic?

Now you can write a number of generic sentences on the board:

The doctor went to the hospital.
The dog bit the man.
The workman held the tool.
The boat crossed the lake.

Go through the sequence starting with *doctor* and *hospital*.

doctor – surgeon – neurosurgeon
hospital – operating room – emergency room

Note: We need to develop some judgment about whether *hospital* reduces logically to *emergency room*. It's permissible to change the prepositional phrase, or object of the verb, in other words the "tale" of the sentence, so long as the basic original meaning is still there. It would be illogical to say:

The neurosurgeon limped to the helicopter.

Of course, this sentence could exist, but this kind of inventiveness is NOT part of our exercise. We need to be disciplined, and to honor the original sentence. We have to remind the students that although we are following rules and indications, we are also engaged in an art, and therefore have various ways to solve the problem. However, the solution has parameters. Judgment is required. When in doubt, be inventive but conservative.

Now ask the students to come up with their own pairs of sentences. You can inspire them with an example or two. These were authored by 8th graders:

generic: The dog ran into the street
specific: The pit bull bolted into the grove.

generic: The boy walked across the road.
specific: The prince strolled across the bridge.

Some class discussion should make it clear that the specific sentence is more interesting, more compelling, more pictorial. Some discussion of the meaning of "generic" is helpful.

Definition: of, applicable to, or referring to all the members of a genus, class, group, or kind; general, not specific.

Noun: a consumer product having no brand name or registered trademark.

Adjective: often used in relation to drugs: having no brand name; not protected by a registered trademark, as in "generic aspirin"

Synonyms: general, common, collective, nonspecific, inclusive, all-encompassing, broad, comprehensive, blanket, umbrella.

Antonym: specific

Origin: late 17th century: from French *générique*, from Latin *genus, gener,* meaning "stock, race."

A conversation about branding would be useful at this point. Purchasing generic products is cost-effective, and there's nothing wrong with it. Big chain stores often have their own generic products:

Safeway has its own organic brand called "O Organics."
Whole Foods' Brand is "365 Everyday Value."
Costco sells its own "Kirkland" brand.

As writers, however, we should stay away from generic words because when we use a specific word, we help the reader see our scene. "The dog ran into the street," for example, is less appealing to the imagination, harder to picture, hence less interesting for the reader, than "The pit bull bolted into the grove." It's always tempting to add modifiers to make the sentence even more specific. If the pit bull is injured and it bolted excitedly and the grove is abandoned, we have even more of a story. True. But our task, at this stage, is to sensitize our students to the power of specificity in the nouns and verbs, without the use of adjectives and adverbs. Later on, when we've disciplined ourselves and have learned to use the most precise words without these assistants, we can lean on them as long as we really need them.

This entire sequence of exercises can constitute the first day's lesson. If there is still time, I often ask the students to do some writing in class. It will help get them immersed in language, help make them feel like writers.

I explain that this is just for me, a sort of "before" example of their writing. I give them the topic: Write a paragraph or two about a place you particularly love. Can you give me a feel of the place? You may NOT introduce a character (human or animal), and you have to leave yourself out of the writing. In other words, don't use "I." It has to be a real place, and you want to describe it as precisely as possible. I keep these examples of the students' writing so that I can see whether there's been improvement by the time we get to the end of our block.

For homework, I might put three generic sentences on the board, have the students copy them, and ask the students to come up with two different specific versions for each example. Next day we'll consider the solutions.

Painless Immersion

Another non-threatening introductory exercise that inevitably leads to laughter while it focuses our attention on vocabulary consists of three-part sentences. Everyone starts with a blank sheet. No need (for once) to write your name at the top.

1. First part of the sentence: the subject
2. Second part of the sentence: a verb
3. Third part of the sentence: an ending (usually a direct object or prepositional phrase, although it is not necessary to name these grammatical details at this point).

Of course, the idea is to avoid a generic word such as "the man" as the subject, and use the most specific word, perhaps "the gardener." Now the paper is passed to the student's neighbor and the second writer has to add a verb. Can we find a verb that is neither boringly obvious nor plainly absurd? What does the gardener do? On the actual paper I still have from such an exercise done with adults, it says, "The gardener teetered." This is a hedge. I mean, anyone can teeter. So let's see whether our third writer redeemed the second writer. The paper is passed again, and something has to be added that takes both the gardener and his teetering into account: "The gardener teetered on the fence top." Yes, that fence top works. It's a bit far-fetched, but we'll let it pass.

Other solutions:

A nurse …	queried …	the priest.
The waitress …	complained …	by coughing.
The skipper …	remembered …	the code.
The biologist …	examined …	his toe.
The Mother Superior …	studied …	the genealogy.

So we started with a nurse, a waitress, a skipper. Our second writer had to come up with an unusual but possible verb: *queried, complained, remembered*. These are interesting. They invite us to complete the sentence. Some thought had to go into the choice of those verbs. What did the skipper remember? The skipper remembered the code. That could be the beginning of a novel. "The waitress complained by coughing" tells us quite a bit about that waitress; "by coughing" was inspired. Not at all what was expected. Of course, we needn't arrive at the unlikeliest conclusion for part three, e.g., "his toe," although doing so will get our attention. Because it was a biologist examining his toe, the sentence has all sorts of potential meaning. Perhaps he was studying some mold. Perhaps he was on a field trip and had stubbed that toe. And without bursting our parameters, the unexpected but possible *toe* introduces an element of humor.

Unless we present this exercise as a vocabulary challenge, the results will quickly deteriorate into absurdity, so the task is to avoid mere silliness. It's harder than it seems, and to raise the bar even more, it can be tried as an oral exercise.

We can then expand this exercise so that each writer produces a whole sentence, and each following writer has to take the previous sentence into account. Again, the following examples come from a class with adults.

> The marathoner collapsed in the heat. Those darn pills.
>   All that training for nothing.
> The toddler scurried to the cupboard. She emptied all the shiny
>   pots and pans and climbed inside. She waited for the proper
>   moment, then popped out with a gleeful hoot.
> The pawnbroker examined the ring. His expression did not
>   change. It was his great-grandmother's.

Later we'll use this effective three-part procedure again.

Alternative Vocabulary

Children love to make lists.

As part of the 7th grade main lesson on Wish, Wonder and Surprise, I often include exercises we can call "Word Choice Vocabulary Lists." If the 8th graders didn't do this exercise in 7th grade, we can do it now. Or we can review it and make new lists. Even adults find such lists revealing.

Finding alternative vocabulary is similar to, but distinct from, the previous exercises dealing with specificity. Here we are not narrowing our choices. Rather, we are finding a broad range of synonyms from which to choose. We are giving ourselves an entire palette of choices.

There are dozens of words we can use instead of *walk*, or the even more generic *go*. The reason there are dozens of words telling us how someone can get from here to there is that there are dozens of ways to get from here to there. Perhaps when the students were in 3rd or 4th grade, they acted out the ways to get from the door to the window: hopping, jumping, skipping, and so forth. We needn't act them all out now, but we do need to realize that our writing will improve by leaps and bounds at a staggering rate if we don't use *go* and *walk* every time we want to show self-locomotion.

We're fortunate in that the English language contains a greater choice of synonyms than many other languages. That's because English consists of words derived from two very different linguistic streams, the Anglo-Saxon on the one hand, and the Latin on the other. For 7th or 8th graders, enough said. For high school students, this is a topic they either have studied or will study in further detail. For adults, we can go into the history of 1066 and all that. The main thing is to realize that the English language, in particular, gives us choices.

Here's a marvelously illustrative poem. I read it to 8th graders, asking them to keep track of the words denoting movement.

> In her nineties and afraid
> of weather and of falling if
> she wandered far outside her door,
> my mother took to strolling in
> the house. Around and round she'd go,
> stalking into corners, backtrack,
> then turn and speed down hallway, stop
> almost at doorways, skirt a table,
> march up to the kitchen sink and
> wheel to left, then swing into
> the bathroom, almost stumble on
> a carpet there. She must have walked
> a hundred miles or more among
> her furniture and family pics,
> mementos of her late husband.
> Exercising heart and limb,
> outwalking stroke, attack, she strode,
> not restless like a lion in zoo,
> but with a purpose and a gait,
> and kept her eyes on heaven's gate.
>
>   – "Heaven's Gate" by Robert Morgan

Because it is a published poem,[7] it will get the students' attention.

Now, how many self-locomotion words did we find? Let's list them: *falling, wandered, strolling,* etc. There are 18! Now we could add to this list with more words of our own.

I ask the students to come up with 10 of their own words for how a person can move from here to there. I start the list on the blackboard, and provide a few more hints:

limp
stagger
stumble
skip

Now we're off and running, and in no time each student has 10 words, and now we collate them into our individual lists. If you don't yet have the word, add it in another color pen. In addition to allowing everyone to come up with a long list of self-locomotion words, this keeps everyone engaged.

run, roll, stagger, dash, trek, stalk, leap, tiptoe, inch, stomp, dance, gallop, skip, wobble, bound, glide, slide, hop, shuffle…

Before you know it, everyone has 60 words, and we stop. Hands continue to pop up, because there are more words—and more. Now that we have this list, let's each come up with some sentences using these words.

Instead of "The man walked across the street," which is a perfectly fine sentence grammatically, we might think about creating an entire story: "The juggler scrambled out of the ring." Why did he scramble? What would happen to this picture if we wrote, "The juggler limped out of the ring"? What are the implications if the juggler "stomped" out of the ring?

Again, it's *important* at this point, still early on in the process, to indicate when the subject and the verb are paired illogically. The point is, can we make a sentence in which we really need the word *shuffle* and not some other way of moving? Who exactly treks? Who shuffles?

In theory, anyone can do any of these actions, but if our imaginations are to be disciplined, then we need to find a logical subject for the verb. We could say a clown treks, or a policeman shuffles, but that would require an entire story to explain, and our sentence needs to make sense on its own. That's the exercise.

So who treks? The adventurer, the hiker, the climber, the Sherpa, the explorer... Just because we're making sense doesn't mean our choices are limited. Who shuffles? Is it a patient, a drunkard, a prisoner ...?

Shackled, the prisoner shuffled out of the courtroom.
Clutching his map, the hiker trekked up the last hill.

For those who want a bigger challenge, let them write something like the poem you read, a poem or paragraph in which the self-locomotion words accrue to add to the picture.

2 Rule Number Two :
Avoid walk *or* go *unless there is no better alternative.*

This would be about the time to raise another red flag. The sentences we've been putting on the board do NOT start with *The*. Starting a sentence with *The* is the most common syntax in English. Common means ordinary, predictable, obvious, b o r i n g . Of course we are allowed to start a sentence with *The*. There's a reason why the *The* syntax is so common. It serves a purpose. But not for now. For now, for the next few days, we are going to try to avoid this common, predictable, obvious, boring syntax, or word order.

3 Rule Number Three: Do not start the sentence with The.

There will be resistance to this. We're in the habit of starting our sentences with *The*. The habit is unfortunately fostered from the early grades on and leads to a formulaic sentence which inevitably, and boringly, begins with *The*. When we ask for an alternative sentence structure, we promote more consciousness about what we do when we write a sentence. Later on we'll allow sentences to start with *The*, though perhaps we'll limit their number to one in every five sentences, or only three to a page, or something like that. Although this sounds like a limitation, it actually fosters creativity because the students can't just resort to the most common, most automatic pattern.

The has a grammatical name: It is the definite article. When we use it, we refer to a *specific* object, instead of any object of its kind. "Excited, the retriever chased the ball" means there is that specific dog chasing that specific ball. That's quite different from "Excited, a retriever chased a ball." When we use *a* or *an* before a noun, it is called the indefinite article, because the thing to which it refers is *any* of its kind, not a specific, definite example of that kind.

4 *Rule Number Four: Rule Number Three therefore also extends to the indefinite article.*

It's helpful to point out, as you read together in class, how a writer finds ways to start a sentence with words other than *The* or *A* or *An*. And while we're on the topic of reading aloud, it's also really supportive to stop and consider a particularly apt word. This becomes more and more influential as our writing goals become more complex. There are some wonderful compilations of exemplary writing in such books as *The Describer's Dictionary: A Treasury of Terms and Literary Quotations for Readers and Writers*, by David Grambs.[6] He has sections on Things, which includes subheadings of Shapes, Patterns and Edges, Surfaces and Textures, Light and Color, among others; Earth and Sky, which includes Terrain and Landscape, Climate, Clouds; Animals; People, which includes Body Types, Frames and Statures, Faces, Eyes, Walk (Gait) and Carriage, and lots of other helpful categories of descriptions. Some of the examples are not useful for children, but many are. Over the years, I have compiled my own set of published examples. It's always impressive for student writers to hear examples by published authors, to show that what we're learning in class translates into real books. Whenever I come across a description of light or water or weather, or find a pithy yet evocative description of a character, I put it in my collection. Very helpful to have examples you yourself have discovered.

Conjunctions, especially the subordinating conjunctions (*moreover, however, whenever, while, because…*) are a writer's friend. They provide a bridge from one phrase to the next and, more importantly for our purpose, from one sentence to the next. Because a sentence that starts with *because* is likely to be more compelling than one which starts with *The* or *A* or *An*, we should have these conjunctions easily accessible in our writing rucksack. Whereas it may not be immediately apparent that stylistically a sentence gains in interest when it doesn't start with *The*, all we have to do is read the average 3rd grader's composition to see that *The* as the beginning of the sentence is ubiquitous. We should be over that by 8th grade, let alone by high school and beyond.

Back to our self-locomotion verbs: As we pick self-locomotion verbs to generate sentences, verbs which are synonyms for the ubiquitous *to go*, we then think of a noun that provides the appropriate subject for that verb, and then determine the setting. Do we think these sentences make sense? I write them on the board starting with *The* and ask for rewrites:

> The jockey limped into the stable. → Limping into the stable, the jockey tended the filly.
> The ballerina slid across the stage. → In her white tutu, the ballerina slid across the stage.

At this point, it's best to be realistic. The next time, tomorrow, we might allow sentences like this:

> Clutching his stomach, the chiropractor staggered into his office.
> Utterly exhausted, the princess crawled the last ten feet.

These sentences are mysterious. It would take many additional sentences to create a context that makes them meaningful instead of merely bizarre, so it's fun to add a few more (but not too many, perhaps three more) to make a story out of it. But now we're getting ahead of ourselves.

Apart from discouraging the merely wild association of words, or a lack of coherence, or a lack of logic, a second challenge is to actually have a gripping story in your one sentence while at the same time avoiding the merely weird. That means we don't want to have a generic subject any more than we want a generic verb. "The boy walked down the street" is the perfect example of a platitude. "The man went to work" is another. *Girl* and *woman* present the same problem.

So let's come up with another list of synonyms: words we can use instead of the generic *boy, girl, man, woman.*

urchin
orphan
toddler

Someone will point out that you can't tell whether *toddler* is a boy or girl. True enough, and we can clarify that in the next sentence with a pronoun. But perhaps we can find words that mean "young male person":

nephew
cadet
altar boy

Hey, that's two words! True enough, but the adjective is really part of the phrase; it's really necessary; we can't find a synonym for this phrase. Let's do this for "young female person":

niece
daughter
schoolgirl

As for words that denote a person, once we provide a few examples, we'll fill the blackboard in no time:

pilot, astronaut, chef, comedian, engineer…
misanthrope, rebel, joker, victim, tourist…

5 Rule Number Five: Avoid using a generic word to denote a human being, unless it's essential.

Now that we have a long list of possible subjects, let's write sentences in which a specific and interesting subject is paired with a fitting self-locomotion verb. The following examples are by 8th graders:

When she found out that someone had eaten her pizza,
Jenna stalked to the door and slammed it behind her.

(Later we'll talk about avoiding names; it's a short cut to avoid finding the right noun.)

With searchlights overhead, the fugitive ducked into the
corner of the abandoned warehouse.

When I read this, I want to know more. *Stalked* and *ducked* are precise and evocative.

Everyone wants to see his or her own sentence on the board. Perhaps three students can come and write their own sentences on the board. It's good to call on people randomly and hear some of the sentences.

Over the next few mornings, we work on other synonym lists:

Words that mean "water":
    ocean, mist, marsh, rill, current, fjord…
We stop at sixty words.

Words that mean "see" or "look":
    notice, glance, gaze, squint…

Words that tell us what light can do:
    beam, glow, spark, flow, flood…

Why do "flow" and "flood" work for water as well as for light? That would be a good topic for conversation.

We should provide repeated opportunities, in class and as homework, for the writing of sentences that use a specific set of synonyms. If we pretend that our sentence is the first sentence of a book, and that this first sentence sets the tone for all that follows, and that this sentence involves some aspect of light, we have a challenge that even the best writers will appreciate, while it inspires those who tend to struggle.

The steep mountains in the east reflect the last golden light of the day.

That was the first line of an 8th grade boy's story entitled "Rain in Death Valley." (Yes, it starts with *The*, but the next sentence doesn't.)

Here is the first line of "Stuck on an Island," a story by an 8th grade girl.

> Golden light stretched up the sky from the east,
> illuminating the fading stars and pale moon.

Ideally, you will return homework number 1 with your comments and corrections on it, before the students do homework number 2. See the section on "Organizing" (page 165) for how to manage the homework flow.

Before long, someone will ask whether you can't ever use a word such as *child*. Of course there's nothing wrong with that word, but when the writer uses it, what does the reader see? It's a very generic word. Eventually, as already noted, we'll use modifiers to flesh out the picture of the child. We'll get to the plague of swarming modifiers in the section on "The Fallacy of the Adjective" (page 114).

For now, though, we should just caution our students, again, that more adjectives do not a better writer make. For mysterious reasons, many students think that the more adjectives they use, the more sophisticated their writing is. On the contrary. We should use modifiers only when we've exhausted the details contained in the noun. We'll come back to this later but because someone will want to add an adjective to these first sentences, it's good to be prepared for why we are trying to avoid them.

6 *Rule Number Six:*
Avoid random adjectives. Rely on the specificity of the noun whenever you can.

To Be, Or Not

A primal linguistic paradox concerns the verb *to be*. Surely this is the most important verb in our language, as without it, we couldn't exist. We might call it the existential verb. Conjugations, declinations and contractions provide disguises; it comes in many forms: *am, are, were, will be*, etc. *Is* is ubiquitous. It's everywhere. And yet, and yet…there is nothing pictorial about it. It *equates*, as in: "16 + 3 is 19." It *declares*, as in: "There's gold in them there hills." Or, grammatically, it *helps*, as in: "During the vacation, we're going to be camping in the Sierras."

Much maligned, mocked and parodied, Edward Bulwer-Lytton's infamous opening line can serve as a caution:

It was a dark and stormy night;…

That's the first phrase. The sentence continues beyond the semi-colon. But these first words have become synonymous with "purple prose" or florid, melodramatic, overwrought writing. Why? What's wrong with it? Nothing, really. And yet, and yet… it is not the best of sentences simply because that formulation, "It was," doesn't captivate the imagination, doesn't originate in the imagination.[8]

[9]

Inexperienced writers will often resort to "It is" or "It was" to start almost any piece of writing. If our goal is to call attention to the advantages of specificity in writing, we should discourage our students from automatically starting with "It is" or "It was" or "There is" or "There was," or for that matter, the plurals: "There are" or "There were."

7 *Rule Number Seven:*
Don't start your sentences with **It is, It was, There is, There was, There are, There were.**

In discussing this rule, I often tell the students about a contest: Since 1982, an annual Bulwer-Lytton Fiction Contest has been sponsored by the English Department of San Jose State University, California. Contestants are required "to compose the opening sentence to the worst of all possible novels."[10]

Even if the students don't quite grasp the pictorial weakness of "It is," etc., the idea that there's a contest for bad writing based on that phrase acts prophylactically.

Word Clusters

Another exercise to enrich and enliven vocabulary is to provide a location (or setting) such as, say, a hairdresser's salon or barbershop; an artist's studio; a grocery store... and then have the students make lists of words that are connected with this place. That might lead us to the following (the locations suggested by students):

Beauty Salon	Farm	Doctor's Office
brush	tractor	stethoscope
hand wall mirrors	irrigation	sphygmomanometer [sic]
clips, pins	hoe	thermometer
comb	silo	examining table
mirror	plow	rubber gloves
blow dryer	cattle	medical microscope
apron	grain	scalpel

Students take to this with a certain amount of glee. Some of them know the specialized vocabulary of working in a bicycle shop or volunteering at the animal shelter.

Now we write sentences, trying to use as many words from one of our groups as we can, without getting silly. It's advisable to keep some gravitas in this exercise, as there is a tendency to be outrageous. Here are some 8th grade results from the groups above:

> Shampoos, conditioners, and oils were stacked on top of
>   cabinets filled with brushes, combs, scissors, clips and pins.
> They use the seeder in the spring. *[My comment on this one was:*
>   *Who is "They"? Where is the picture?]*
> Listening through the stethoscope, the pediatrician heard the
>   infant's heartbeat.

Just about now, we need to put some constraints on what's allowed, or we're in danger of getting inappropriate, garish, grotesque, lurid or lewd sentences. It's time to introduce the "Avoid List."

The Avoid List

At this point, when the students are coming up with their sentences, someone will offer something like this:

Harry Potter flew at a million miles an hour to catch the snitch.

This provides the perfect springboard for the Avoid List.

It's essential that we set forth some fundamentals for the type of writing we're interested in. I simply make a list on the side of the board and keep it there throughout the main lesson block. (If we're teaching a track class, it's advisable to have the handwritten list on a poster on the wall by the board.)

I also have our Rules listed in a conspicuous place. I ask a student to be our Rules Secretary and to add to it as we generate new rules.

Inevitably, the need for the Avoid List arises soon after we start making our sentences because someone is sure to use content that I disqualify. Needless to say, there is pushback about my Avoid List, but I explain that the reason we are avoiding certain types of writing is because those types of writing are too easy for us. If you are in the realm of science fiction or fantasy, anything goes, whereas what we are learning here, is how to describe a world that is actually possible. We are training our imaginations, not letting them go wild. This is a difficult concept even for adults, but at this point I often mention that the people who find our Pictorial Writing method to be most useful are those involved in scientific writing. I quote a high school physics teacher, who, after having to submit to the rules and exercises in an adults' creative writing class, confided that he had finally learned a method for getting his students to write objectively, precisely, and in detail as they describe their physics experiments. That was high praise.

It's advantageous to involve the students in making the Avoid List. They usually get the drift quickly, and we add to the list as the need arises. (This list is about content. We articulate the stylistic or grammatical Avoids as Rules.)

The Avoid List
science fiction
fantasy
anything bizarre
violence
magic
fairy tale
shock
dream
proper names

If I have the courage of my convictions about this, I find that the tasks we are working on are compelling enough, with a high enough bar, a high enough degree of difficulty that students let go of their sci-fi, fairy-tale worlds pretty easily.

Creative Writing

8th Grade 2016

Teacher: Ms. Winter

A Story in One Sentence

So far we've 1) established the importance of *choosing* our words to help the reader see what we, as writers, are describing; 2) broadened the choices of subjects and verbs of self-locomotion; and 3) learned to avoid starting the sentence with *The*. Now we can work on firing up the writer's, and thus the reader's, imagination.

To start us off with the Story in One Sentence—which we already practiced, but did not name as such, when we came up with sentences like "Shackled, the prisoner shuffled out of the courtroom" or "Clutching his map, the hiker trekked up the last hill"—I might provide some new examples:

Unable to retrieve his oar, the rower watched the approaching maelstrom.

or:

Idly strolling along the surf's edge, the couple lost sight of their Border Collie.

Of course there will be a clever person who says, "But that could be the beginning of a story, too." Yes, any sentence can be developed with a second sentence, and soon enough we are going to be writing a Story in Three Sentences. And after that we'll be writing longer short stories. But for now we're practicing to create pictures which reveal a whole scenario, which quickly engages us so that we want to know more.

We work on coming up with sentences that utilize our earlier lessons and have the goal of being stories-in-one-sentence. That means we'll have a specific, non-generic subject, and our verb will be an alternative to the generic *walk* or *go*. We want to write a sentence which allows us to grasp an entire scenario. Each sentence has one very specific subject and a perfect verb and provides a context. Here are some solutions by 8th graders:

> The orphan tiptoed out of his bedroom and into the hallway.
> *[Yes, it starts with "The" but "orphan tiptoed" makes up for it.]*

> In the early morning, the widow crept out of the thatched hut.

> She sang as she waltzed happily around the house.

True, *house* is generic, but the rest of the sentence permits its use. To reiterate: It's important for students to realize that writing is an art and that, although there are rules and suggestions, each of us must make our own decisions about what works or doesn't work. In this sentence, *house* works. In the previous sentence, *thatched hut* is essential, and far more evocative than *house*. What works in one sentence doesn't necessarily work in another.

> As the band strolled on stage, the fans howled and shrieked while stomping their feet and waving and clapping their hands.
> Inching toward the dishwasher, he complained loudly about how he had already washed all the dishes that day.

The picture is so precise, that the generic *he* is acceptable. Could we improve the sentence by making him more specific? What about *the teenager*?

> After four days of their parents' absence, the twins began to worry.

Yes, that works. *Twins* is good choice. I can immediately imagine various circumstances. *Twins* is a more evocative by far than *children*.

> He seemed unable to cope with the load of books.

Oh, oh. Who is "he"? The student? The professor? The librarian? Furthermore, that last example brings up the next rule:

8 *Rule Number Eight:* *Avoid using the word* **seems** *or* **appears**. *Be author-itative.*

When writers use *seems* or *appears*, as in "appears to be," they are usually hedging their bets. We spend some time in class considering situations in which *seems* might be used legitimately, i.e., because it's really needed, rather than because the writer is unsure. As writers we should be authoritative. Author-itative!

Fundamental Principle Number One:
Use the students' examples as a guide for what needs further work.

If a student uses *seems*, that's your reason to bring up the rule about it. If a student uses profanity, a new rule must be added.

Start with a Particular, Specific, Concrete Word

Once the basics have been established, and the students are beginning to get that we can't just write down the first word that comes to mind, and that the reader should see what we are describing, we can get a lot of mileage out of an exercise that starts with a single word. We provide a word, just one, and ask the students to write a story in one sentence. Of course the sentence must contain the word.

The students will have plenty of suggestions, and this is a good way to make sure that the provided word is the most specific variable. *Vehicle*, for example, would not be as good as *tractor*. What about *Porsche Panamera SE-Hybrid*? This could give rise to another rule:

9 *Rule Number Nine:*
Use proper nouns cautiously.

For example, if you use a proper name for a character, you might feel that no other identifying features are necessary. So it can be a lazy person's shortcut, and we are trying to avoid those. However, in some sentences, the specific make and model of a car might be just perfect. Again, it's a matter of developing some judgment. Students generally like that, and it works as long as you, the teacher, are the ultimate judge.

10 *Rule Number Ten:*
Avoid proper names for the characters
unless you have many additional details.

But let's get back to our one word: If the chosen word is *tractor*, we would then want a sentence in which the word *tractor* is so desirable that no other type of vehicle would do.

> In the middle of the potato field, the tractor sputtered to a halt.

Someone might argue that it could have been a Land Rover that sputtered to a halt in the potato field, and so it could. But the real question is whether the setting supports the key word, and it does. And *sputtered* is a good choice. So it works. How about the word *violin*?

> After the concert, the musician left her violin on the bus.

Why is that not so good? Why is this better:

> After the concert, the concert mistress carefully put her priceless violin back into its case.

Because *the musician* is less precise than *concert mistress*, and because it is less precise, we could substitute *trombone* in that first sentence without changing anything else in the sentence. We could not substitute *trombone* in the second sentence. Note that the adjective *priceless* is essential, not mere filigree. We can use this type of exercise as a quick warm-up at the start of our work.

Fundamental Principle Number Two:
No work, whether homework or class work, may be discarded.
(See section on "Tracking and Evaluating," page 167)

8th Grade

January 2016

CREATIVE WRITING

Ms. Winter

A Story in Three Sentences

After harvesting and scrutinizing the stories-in-one-sentence which were written for homework, we're ready to up the ante with a story in three sentences.

A good way to move from the one-sentence-story to the three-sentence-story is to ask the students to take their favorite homework story-in-one-sentence and expand on it. Of course each of the new sentences needs to follow the rules and guidelines we've established already.

Don't start with *The*.
Specific vocabulary.
Avoid the Avoid List.
And especially important: Each sentence has to be a picture.

While there are those who might find this exercise daunting or tiresome, one or two who finish quickly might be asked to put their sentences on the board. Here is an example from an 8th grader who wrote easily.

As he looked at the horizon, the sailor caught a glimpse of a storm. While he watched, the clouds grew and came closer and waves became choppy. Suddenly, he saw a break in the cloud cover and somehow, with all his strength, managed to hold on to his boat and reach the calm water.

Because it's still early in the main lesson, I wouldn't indicate the weaknesses to the student, but were I to do so, I might return the paragraph looking like this. "Caught a glimpse" is circled because you don't really catch a glimpse of a storm. What exactly alerted him to the coming storm? Clouds "grew and came closer" is circled because the clouds probably did not grow and come closer. Perhaps the writer is thinking of fog. "Suddenly" is discussed below. "Somehow" is vague as vague can be. And I really want to know how the sailor was able to "hold on to his boat." Granted, this writer was hampered by the task of writing only three sentences, but that's no excuse. We have to manage the restrictions of our exercises without resorting to weak writing.

> As he looked at the horizon, the sailor caught a glimpse of a storm. While he watched, the clouds grew and came closer and waves became choppy. Suddenly he saw a break in the cloud cover and somehow, with all his strength, managed to hold on to his boat and reach the calm water.

If this example were on the blackboard, I would use the occasion to add a new item to our Avoid List.

11 Rule Number Eleven: *Avoid* suddenly, all of a sudden, unexpectedly.

When a writer uses *suddenly* or *all of a sudden*, it usually means that the writer is looking for a mindless solution to how to go on. Usually, the word *suddenly* is an easy fix. Anything can be "sudden."

Far better to give a hint of what was sudden. In the sentence above, why did the sailor notice the cloud cover? Of course, *suddenly* is a perfectly good word, but it shouldn't be used like caulk, to patch sentences together. If something really does occur "suddenly," by all means let's use *suddenly*.

This can become a separate exercise. Perhaps the teacher can provide examples of sentences using *suddenly,* and the students can determine whether it's a justified use or a lazy use.

> During the performance, an overhead stage light suddenly
>   fell onto the set.
> Suddenly, it began to rain.
> When the car ahead suddenly swerved, we were lucky that it
>   didn't hit anything.
> Suddenly the door opened and a clown unexpectedly walked
>   into the party.
> Hiking up the steep trail, we suddenly decided to stop for lunch.

Each of these sentences can be discussed. It's good if the students get involved in the actual content, the meaning, of each sentence. There might be differences of opinion. Do you, in fact, suddenly decide to stop for lunch while hiking up a steep trail? Depending on the circumstances, this *suddenly* might be justified. The point is: Don't use *suddenly* without thinking about it.

We can practice our Three-Sentence-Stories in various other ways: Each student writes a sentence, folds the paper so that sentence can't be seen, and passes it along to the next student. It's been my experience that no matter how strict the parameters for this exercise, inevitably it becomes hilarious. So be prepared for some comic relief. In any event, it's important to provide instructions for that first sentence, so that all of us are working within the same framework, and we have some basis for comparison. We might ask that the first sentence describe some place on the school campus, for example. If there is a prominent local geographical point of interest such as a lake, mountain, park or trail, we might start there. Because the train of thought instigated by an outdoor setting is usually more salubrious than one starting indoors, I insist that the setting be a place in nature.

Again, we have to remind our student writers of the rules:

Don't start with *The*.
Use specific vocabulary.
Avoid the Avoid List.
Pictures!

I tell the students that the point of the exercise is to put yourself into the picture of the first sentence and to bring a character into the sentence that makes sense. Then, the action the character performs must be integral to the setting and the character. Finally, an ending sentence. Inevitably, humor replaces reason in this exercise, so it is also possible to throw caution to the winds and allow for funny non-sequiturs.

Having the sequence spelled out on the board is helpful, and we might choose any of the following, depending on how we've worked up to this moment.

1. Location or Setting (in nature)
2. Character
3. Action and Conclusion

This can also look like this:
1. Location or Setting (in nature)
2. Character and Action
3. Conclusion

Or we could expand into:
1. Location or Setting (in nature)
2. Character
3. Action
4. Conclusion

This sequence is going to become important later on, so it's helpful if we really understand each category and, therefore, it's good to spend a bit of time elaborating on the ingredients.

1. To mitigate the challenge of an imagined-but-true scene, I limit the setting to a place in nature. I've found that if I fail to do this, settings tend to the dark side. I want to discourage stories taking place in basements or attics, in restaurants or bowling alleys. That can come later, much later, in high school and beyond.
2. The character must be human. Later we can add a second character, and that second character might even be an animal. Providing this parameter limits the sentimentality which animals so easily inflict. Avoiding a second human character eliminates obvious dramas.
3. By action, I simply mean, what did the character do? It doesn't have to be a great, big, earth-shattering action; it can be small and subtle.
4. Conclusion means: Find a way to end it.

James's Story

In preparing the students for this sequence, I might well read the following story by a boy who was an 8th grader some 40 years ago! He's now an internationally known oceanographer, Professor James Leichter (he agreed to be identified), at the Scripps Institution of Oceanography in San Diego. I read the story from a published booklet, which gives it clout.

A Moment on a Mountain Stream

Cold clear water sparkled over the rocks, while little silvery minnows darted around a pool in a trickling mountain stream. The sunlight flashing through the water made wave-like patterns on the rocky stream bed. About ten yards upstream a young pine tree bowed into the water, as if it were drinking, but as the breeze let up, the tree sprang out of the water, leaving a trail of pine needles floating downstream. Dead leaves bobbed up and down in the current and raced little twigs downstream. Along the mossy shoreline, scrawny brown mushrooms were pushing through the fall's cover of dead leaves while a rotting log was providing a field day for ants and other insects. All the while, the lush green trees quivered in the lazy breeze.

With a crackling of twigs, a long fly fishing rod was thrust out from behind a bush. A tall, thin fisherman followed close behind, and almost fell as he crossed over the marshy grasses. The fisherman stretched out a little line and started to cast. After a few casts, a nine pound rainbow trout darted out from under a rock, heading straight for the cast fly. As the fish reached the fly, the water boiled behind him but he suddenly turned and shot back to the rock's safety.

This continued for about twenty minutes, until on one cast, the fish rocketed through the water, taking the fly with him. After a long struggle, the fisherman pulled the exhausted fish to a net. The fisherman held up his glittering trophy, the nine pound trout, but seeing what a beautiful fish it was, he decided to release his catch.

The fish quivered in the water for a few seconds, and then, slowly but smoothly swam back to his home under the rock. Meanwhile, the fisherman secured his line, put his creel over his shoulder and stumbled away through the lush vegetation. In a few minutes he returned, having forgotten a small plastic tackle box. As he again left the stream, he first got his fishing rod tangled in a tree, and then dropped his tackle box, and generally left the fishing spot in a much less graceful manner than the fish had.[11]

This story by a talented youngster was the culmination of many, many lessons and lots of practice. In those days, I hadn't yet formulated the "pictorial method." Nevertheless, good writing is good writing, and even back then we practiced economy, precision and detail. Reading this story aloud in preparation of our sentence-passing exercise will inspire our current crop of incipient writers; it sets the bar high. True, this is a story in four paragraphs, not in three sentences, but there is such clarity of sequence that it demonstrates the effectiveness of our outline.

I recently got in touch with James. Here is what he said about those 8th grade days:

I don't recall writing the specific story about the fisherman, but reading it again was fun and even all these years later I can recall and visualize pretty much exactly what I was imagining at the time—that fantasy scene all was set in a very specific, real location of the little stream down the hill from our family vacation farm in Vermont. It's a spot that I did go and try fishing in those years—although the most I would ever have caught was a couple small perch and nothing like a giant, salmon-sized trout. What a fantastical tale that was…! So, I think one of the positive things about that essay experience was that you encouraged us to visualize real places and then add in the elements of fantasy freely.

What our middle-aged oceanographer doesn't mention is the prescience of his story which lies in its sensitive, empathetic and precise observation of nature. His musicality (he played French horn in our 8th grade orchestra) is also evident in the cadence of his sentences. In his recent letter to me, James included the following recollection:

What I remember about the writing projects in 7th/8th grades is not the specifics but that we did do quite a bit of writing and there was a big jump in expectations/quality compared to the earlier grades. I think we also started to have real homework and that you pushed and encouraged us fairly strongly which I appreciate (now looking back, and I think even at the time). I recall that we did both writing and rewriting of essays in those years, and I think that was a particularly useful skill to develop. I recall also that we really dug into grammar, and I recall that being very useful. I recall that 7th grade was when we really started to learn the language in a more structured way.

James confessed:

I was a "slow" start at reading. I really didn't get it at all in the 1st, 2nd, and even 3rd grades. I recall the feeling when I was probably 7 or 8 years old that some of the other kids were much advanced and I wondered if I'd ever really be able to read(!). And then sometime in 4th grade it all clicked and I was off and into a lot of great adventure books (things like the "Little House" series, "Phantom Tollbooth," "Lion Witch Wardrobe" series, "Hardy Boys," and all that stuff). But I've sometimes wondered if I were a kid now in these accelerated times or had been at a school that pushed early reading if I might have lost my confidence and adopted some kind of label like a "slow reader" and how my subsequent experiences in school might, or might not, have all been different. Anyway, by 7th/8th grades it was all pretty natural to me, and I do recall that I liked reading and writing quite well.

James was an exceptionally able student by the time I met him when I took over the class in 7th grade. He was the youngest of three, and his two older brothers who had preceded him at the Rudolf Steiner School in New York City, also excelled at just about anything they tried. They played sports; they played instruments; they were ambitious and energetic.

James continues his narrative, and because he excelled in both the sciences and humanities, and thus represents a truly "Waldorfian" quality, I think it's worth including the rest of his story:

Then on to High School and the two topics I really enjoyed (and actually did my homework—unlike other topics—ha!) were English and Biology. I was always good at Math but never loved that as much. There was a direct connection from the ways you had taught us English and writing to the ways Ekkehard Piening did so, and the aspects of verbal narrative and imagination were very influential. I went on in college at Stanford to study Biology, but then actually majored in English—mainly because Stanford had an overseas study program at Oxford and priority of the applications went to English majors. At Oxford it was possible to study at a very high level and take part in the Oxford tutorial system, with weekly one-on-one or two-to-one hour-long meetings with the faculty tutors. That was a great experience relative to anything I'd had in the first two years of college, with mostly large and impersonal classes. I think, also that in many ways I was prepared for that experience from the Steiner years where the school and classes were so small that essentially it was all close interactions with the faculty. There was very little hiding behind the group any time through the Steiner experience!

Note: The "Steiner experience" prepared him for his Oxford tutorials! His interest in writing morphed:

Once I found my way to Stanford's marine lab in Monterey the dice were pretty quickly cast in terms of the field I ended up pursuing. I got a Masters at Northeastern University in Boston and after that received a fellowship from NSF [the National Science Foundation] that supported my PhD which I pursued back at Stanford and in Monterey. From there it was on to Woods Hole for a postdoc and then an Assistant Professor job offer at Scripps in San Diego, which I took almost site-unseen [sic] and in retrospect very naively. Well, that's the story—and the connection is that really I think of myself very much as a professional writer. I'm writing manuscripts for publication, grant proposals, reports, and all sorts of other documents all the time. And, I can tell you one of the things that has really pleased me is when I've had people say that my papers are well-written. So, YES, it's all a meandering and sometimes dotted line, but I really do think my writing goes all the way back to days at the Steiner School and High School.

It took several weeks for my request to James to yield results. As he wrote at the beginning of his reflections:

I became quite busy here in Tokyo with various work and meetings, and preparing for our field work which is starting this week—weather permitting. In any case, here are some thoughts on your questions below, now while I'm on a flight to Ishigaki.

The Beach and the Forest

After the "pass the paper" exercise, I collect the papers, and read them aloud. Since the writing is anonymous, I can comment, as needed, on what works well or not so well. I might read several examples, and then ask where we have the strongest picture. Inevitably, there'll be a consensus. QED.

Now that we have benefited from the constraint and discipline of counting our sentences, we can move to the idea of a paragraph. (The section on paragraphs follows, and of course depending on the teacher's inclinations, the paragraph per se might be the next subject. I find that it's more fruitful to get into the *what* before I tackle the *how*.) I ask the students to choose one of two settings.

Remarkably, providing the setting in no way hampers the imagination. On the contrary, for those who get confused by the "blank canvas," the provided setting is reassuring. By providing a springboard, as it were, we liberate the writer, who can now focus on the "what" instead of getting hung up on the "where." Very soon now, we're going to write a story without provided constraints. There will be no guardrails. For now, though, we're still going to work off of given suggestions.

In the San Francisco Bay Area, where I last taught this creative writing block, I suggested one of two well-known local places. The students could choose to describe either a beach scene or the top of Mt. Tamalpais, known locally as Mt. Tam, the highest peak in the Bay Area. In the end, all students will have written about both places, but along with the liberation of not counting sentences, the additional liberation of having a choice, even if it was between only two things, was welcome. When giving the assignment, either as homework or as an in-class exercise, I remind the students of the rules we've already absorbed:

> Don't start with *The*.
> Use specific vocabulary.
> Avoid the Avoid List.
> Pictures!

Here are some student examples (names have been changed):

> Thick, heavy fog surrounded Mt. Tam, the highest mountain peak in Marin County, California, on this overcast day. As the snow-like fog starts to drift away from the summit, one could see that there are actually two peaks, one a bit taller than the other. Covered with wild life, lakes and waterfalls, native plants and hiking trails, this mountain is a fantastic place to spend the day. (Aishe)

> It is a clear, windy day on Mt. Tam, and the sun does little to warm the crisp air. The slopes of the mountain are golden-brown, with jade-colored clusters of oaks and laurels. Far below, the bay glitters and reflects the sunlight, while further south a thin blanket of fog lies low in the sky. Deep redwood forests cover entire valleys, with plunging cliffs that drop to the sea. Miles and miles of the land and sea below stretch on until they fade into the haze of the horizon. (Fionghoula)

Climbing to the overcast sky, the path winds around a golden hill. Sparkling droplets of the first rain of the season cling to the yellow grasses. Deep green woods creep up the valley, threatening to overtake the meadow. The crest of the hill looks out over almost the entire bay area *[sic]*. The clouds are high enough to reveal Sutro tower dissapearing *[sic]* into the thick fog billowing over San Francisco. (Sheryl)

Spots of dappled light hit the spongy forest floor, while overhead, the tops of the majestic trees seem to point onward into infinity. The faint sap-like aroma fills the chilling morning air and a gentle breeze brings the mists from the valley. All would be silent, if it were not for the chattering squirrels and occasional hawk's cry. (Phineas)

It's six o'clock in the morning and the top most third of Mt. Tam is covered in a thick cloud of fog and mist The sun is just starting to rise over the horizon which is creating a beautiful and large assortments of reds, and oranges and pinks in the sky. There is no wind and the trees and bushes lay as still as a house. In the distance, birds are starting to wake up and chirp their morning songs. On the paths of mount Tam lie little creeklets of water from the mist. All is still, but will come alive very soon. *[with original errors]* (Ju-Ri)

The first example is by an athletic girl, one of those rare teenagers where "what you see is what you get." She enjoys participating in local theater, singing, dancing and acting. Imagination is a foreign country for her, and she is more comfortable with the facts. Consequently, the pictures are fuzzy. Because we were still in the early stages of learning to write in pictures, I didn't point out all the shortcomings, but if this were an advanced class, there might be a number of comments:

> Thick, heavy fog surrounded *[I underline with a squiggly line to indicate that something is wrong with the word—in this case, the fog did not "surround" the mountain]* Mt. Tam, the highest mountain peak in Marin County, California, on this overcast *[Do we need to say it's "overcast" if we've already provided "heavy fog"]* day. As the snow-like fog starts *[What is "snow-like fog"?]* to drift away from the summit, one *[This impersonal pronoun is her means of sticking to the rule to avoid bringing in a character at this stage—so it is a kind of cheating of that rule]* could see that there are actually two peaks, one a bit taller than the other. Covered with wild life, lakes, and waterfalls, native plants and hiking trails, this mountain is a fantastic place to spend the day. *[She concludes her recital of facts with a heartfelt exclamation, as if she senses that just the facts are not enough.]* (A)

Three weeks later, this girl had made real progress in picturing the events, rather than providing information. Here is the beginning of one of her final short stories:

> Fair music buzzed in the background as people chattered away on Sunday morning at the Farmers' Market. Rows of white tents, offering everything from fruits and vegetables to farm fresh dairy products, covered the grounds. The whirring hum of industrial blenders cranked out rainbow-colored smoothies. People swarmed to order one before the smoothie vendor sold out.

It's not perfect. We still have the generic words—*people, fruits, vegetables, dairy products*—but we also have specific verbs such as *buzz* and *chatter*, *crank* and *swarm*. Her story was about Tucker, who "was known all over Marin County for his unique sandwich combinations and his deep tenor voice." She is "into" her story.

Our next example is by a quiet, confident girl who loves to write, and was, as I found out after our main lesson was over, writing a novel set in ancient Rome for her 8th grade project.

It is *[If I haven't yet pointed out to the students that we try to avoid "it is" because it always indicates a fact, an equation, rather than a picture, I would do so now, and add it to the Avoid List on the basis of finding it here]* a clear, windy day on Mt. Tam, and the sun does little to warm the crisp air. *[Would we call moving air "crisp"?]* The slopes of the mountain are golden-brown, with jade-colored *["jade" is nice]* clusters of oaks and laurels. Far below *[Evidently, the first line describes the summit, but we don't know that, so "far below" is a bit confusing.]*, the bay glitters and reflects the sunlight, while further south a thin blanket of fog *[Because we are dealing here with a good student, I might use this "blanket of fog" to bring in the whole realm of simile, metaphor and cliché.]* lies low in the sky. *[lies "low" in the "sky"?]* Deep redwood forests cover entire valleys *[How does this mesh with the golden-brown slopes?]*, with plunging cliffs that drop to the sea *[The point of view is unsteady—where is the writer located? What is the point of view?]* Miles and miles of the land and sea below stretch on until they fade into the haze of the horizon. (F)

Glib. Unpenetrated. Are both land and sea "below"? What haze? Where is the fog now? Horizon?

Her novel is well-conceived and well-crafted. A lot of research and effort went into it. It could easily become a reader for 6th grade main lessons on Rome. Not only did I NOT know she was working on it during our creative writing block, I also was unable to attend her project presentation. Later I heard that she acknowledged our recent 8th grade work with the following words:

> I would like to thank Ms. Winter for giving me the confidence to take my creative writing to a whole new level. Although I had long wanted to write a book, I would not have accomplished it at this point in my life without Ms. Winter's teaching and inspiration. She helped me learn to develop characters and scenes as if I were drawing pictures with words, and taught me how to fashion the trajectory of a plot or story so that it flows naturally to its conclusion.

I include the acknowledgment, at the risk of apparent self-flattery, because her phrase, "drawing pictures with words" is so apt. She got it! I expect that she will continue to Write On!

The third example also comes from a confident girl, fluent in Portuguese, a surfer, and a very able student. She told me she was more interested in science than in writing. Naturally, I took pains to impress upon her the "science" of imaginative writing. You can't just make it up.

> Climbing to the overcast sky, the path winds around a golden hill. *[If the path is winding around a hill, can it be climbing to the sky; and is it really climbing to the sky?]* Sparkling droplets *[Would the droplets be sparkling if it was overcast?]* of the first rain of *[Let's try to avoid the "of... of" repetition.]* the season cling to the yellow grasses. Deep

green woods creep up the valley, threatening to overtake the meadow. *["Threatening" is a bit much, but the writer is trying to enliven the description, and by using "creep" she was able to avoid a more static verb, such as "lie."]* The crest of the hill looks out *[Personification! Now we need to add it to our Avoid List.]* over almost the entire bay area *[sic]*. The clouds are high enough to reveal Sutro tower dissapearing *[sic]* into the thick fog billowing over San Francisco. (S)

This girl's first draft for this paragraph began like this:

Midnight moonlight streamed through the redwood canopy, illuminating the huge trunks and curling ferns. A trickling stream disrupted the cold silence.

That was a good start, and I'm not sure why she dropped it. Frequently, the spontaneous in-class version of a task that was subsequently assigned as homework proves to be preferable.

Then, the work of a young man who writes with ease and has a very good grasp of the mechanics. Punctuation, spelling, grammar… no problem. He was able to "get" the instructions for improving his writing and got engaged in the process of solving the problems I provided.

Spots of dappled light hit the spongy forest floor, while overhead, the tops of the majestic trees seem *[Do they or don't they?]* to point onward into infinity. *[Perhaps the "seem" is because of the dubious choice of "infinity."]* The *[Shouldn't this be "A"?]* faint sap-like aroma fills the chilling morning air and a gentle breeze brings the mists from the valley. *[Is this meteorologically true? Can the air be "chilling" and moving in a "gentle breeze"?]* All would be silent, if it were not for the chattering squirrels and occasional hawk's cry. *[This is a nice touch, bringing in the animals, especially if we haven't barred them from this assignment.]* (P)

Finally, a piece of evocative, heartfelt, poetic, soulful writing by a young man who often arrived to class late, had trouble keeping track of his work, was a bit cheeky until he found out that didn't work with me, and ended up writing some meaningful stories.

It's six o'clock in the morning and the top most third of Mt. Tam is covered in a thick cloud of fog and mist The *[He was our run-on champion!]* sun is just starting to rise over the horizon which is creating a beautiful and large assortments of reds, and oranges and pinks in the sky. There is no wind and the trees and bushes lay *[sic]* as still as a house. In the distance, birds are starting to wake up and chirp their morning songs. On the paths of mount Tam lie little creeklets of water from the mist. All is still, but will come alive very soon. (J)

This is the perfect time to offer two separate evaluations, one for the mechanics, because by now we really ought to avoid run-on sentences, and one for the remarkably clear-eyed and sensitive picture. He has an ear for cadence, and the final sentence is prescient of his own state.

From all the writing harvested by means of this exercise, I would extract our next topics. I would read some examples aloud and point out how the problems can be overcome. For example, that "blanket of fog" … it's the perfect example of a tired, listless, lazy, clichéd phrase.

Over the years, I've often told my writing students (whatever their ages) that whenever I come across a "red apple," I lose my appetite. But more of this later.

In addition to the paragraphs about Mt. Tam, each student also wrote a paragraph describing a beach. Here is Phineas's:

> In the west the sun is setting over the rolling fog, and in the east the least light is shining over the hills. The gray sand is damp and cold from the salty waves of the recent high tide. A slight breeze is rustling the dune grasses and shrubs, while out on the water the wind is creating white caps and a mist off the sea.

This is an exact description, yet it doesn't fall into mere information. This student has a sense for melody in his writing, which carries the description. If I wanted to be picky, I might point out the plethora of adjective-noun bundles: rolling fog, gray sand, salty waves, recent high tide, slight breeze, dune grasses, white caps. Perhaps I would write a comment on his paper, indicating that he could change some of these adjective-noun combos. I might also take the opportunity to point out to the class that using the continuous tense is not necessary, and that Phineas would have strengthened his paragraph had he written:

> In the west the sun <u>sets</u> over the rolling fog, and in the east the least light <u>shines</u> over the hills. The gray sand is damp and cold from the salty waves of the recent high tide. *[Here the "is" is not part of the verb.]* A slight breeze <u>rustles</u> the dune grasses and shrubs, while out on the water the wind <u>creates</u> white caps and a mist off the sea.

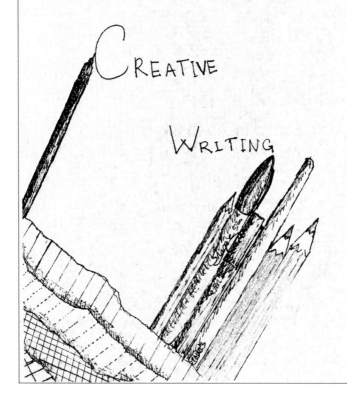

CAMILA KILLION
JANUARY 2016
EIGHTH GRADE
M.S. WINTER

CREATIVE

WRITING

A Paragraph

Having now thrown the students "into the deep end" as is my wont, by having them write paragraphs without preparing them for the niceties of paragraphs as opposed to sentences, we now tackle the paragraph more consciously.

Left to their own devices, students often lack a paragraph sense. Sentence-sense, which enables the student to avoid run-on sentences and sentence fragments, deserves its own discussion and will be part of the section on grammar.

We've already stitched sentences together into the Three-Sentence-Story, and we've used several integrated and connected sentences to describe a beach and a forest. But the purpose of those sentences was to engage the imagination so that rather than stop at the end of the first sentence, we could expand and develop our story with further pictures.

Crafting a paragraph is not the same as stringing sentences together. It's time to work on how to get from one sentence to the next, one paragraph to the next.

Transitions

Transitions have found favor with students of all ages. 7th and 8th graders are among the most appreciative. When asked, at the end of our block, to name what they found most useful, many students, whether weak or strong writers, mentioned transitions. They liked the "science" of building bridges between sentences. Taking the themes of beach and forest which we used for homework, I now provide the students with a first sentence:

> From the ridge of the mountain, fog rolled down toward the redwoods.

I ask the students to add one sentence to this picture. The task is to make sure that the second sentence is predicated on the first. Is there a clue in the first sentence which leads to the second? In the sentence above, for example, we have the mountain ridge, the fog, and the redwoods. Our second sentence should therefore pick up on one of these "clues." We consider the following, which I provide or solicit from the students, and look at which word in the first sentence develops further in the second sentence.

> From the ridge of the mountain, fog rolled down toward the redwoods. Bare boulders lay scattered along the mountain's spine.

In this continuation of the first sentence, "ridge" is the clue, and it leads to the picture of the mountain's spine.

> From the ridge of the mountain, fog rolled down toward the redwoods. Thick and wet, the fog enveloped every rock and tree.

In this solution, we took "fog" as the clue, and we added details about the fog.

From the ridge of the mountain, fog rolled down toward the redwoods. Their trunks reached up and disappeared in the dense fog.

Our third variation took *redwoods* as the clue, and we work with them. It's up to us to decide which part of the picture we'll take as our clue, and how we'll expand on it.

Having explained the exercise, I now write a sentence on the board, and ask the students to copy it, label it as (1) and continue with two variations of a second sentence, each labeled (2). Here are some of the results:

Great waves pounded the sand. By the dunes, many animal tracks ran in all directions.

Great waves pounded the sand. They washed up the creek, snaking beneath the tall billowing grasses.

Great waves pounded the sand. Through the break of every wave, porpoises playfully dove in and out.

Perhaps you can tell that these second sentences are not really penetrated with imagination. In the first sentence, the dunes seem like a logical extension of "sand," but the sand in the first sentence is wet, whereas the dunes in the second sentence are dry. And: Is there an inherent connection between great waves pounding the sand and animal tracks running in all directions? Maybe, but it would need to be explained.

In the second variation, the waves wash up the creek. That's okay. But then the imagination ebbs, and the waves snake on beneath tall billowing grasses. Is that likely? As for the porpoises, they're nice, but the first sentence does not really give rise to them. They're just convenient.

I've found that it usually takes several days to get this idea of transitions across. I try to create as many different ways of working at it as I can—without overdoing it.

One exercise that works well is for me to provide the beginning of a story which the students are then asked to complete in class. There is usually a time limit of 15 or 20 minutes. Of course one of the intriguing aspects of this exercise is that there is considerable variety in the "solution" of the continuation. Part of the task is to bring a character into the setting and then find some sort of appropriate conclusion to the story. Here is one such beginning which I provided:

> As true as a mirror, the flat pond perfectly reflected the distant forests in their autumn hues of gold and crimson. A merganser landed feet first fragmenting the image of forests, hills and sky. Soon a second duck followed. They dove and surfaced, dove and surfaced, as if they had all day. Indeed, the picnic tables in the grove were empty yet, and the early morning frost still streaked their surfaces. A blue jay hopped about looking for a morsel fallen from a plate. Crows flapped and croaked in the trees.

After having the students read this to themselves, I asked them to take a pencil and to indicate with circled words and arrows, the various transitions already provided.

As true as a mirror, the flat pond perfectly reflected the distant forests in their autumn hues of gold and crimson. A merganser landed feet first fragmenting the image of forests, hills and sky. Soon a second duck followed. They dove and surfaced, dove and surfaced, as if they had all day. Indeed, the picnic tables in the grove were empty yet, and the early morning frost still streaked their surfaces. A blue jay hopped about looking for a morsel fallen from a plate. Crows flapped and croaked in the trees.

Having reminded them of how transitions are part of the invisible skeleton keeping the picture together in a piece of writing, I ask them to continue the setting for a sentence or two, before introducing a character. Additional animals are not allowed. (The inexperienced writer will become wrapped up with the puppy or deer and lose sight of the actual task of the exercise.) Here are several continuations, provided by 8th graders:

> A squirrel chattered a warning around mid-morning, and then darted into the safe hollow of a tree. The mergansers paddled away uneasily, and the blue jay soared to a high viewing spot in a broad oak with the crows.

You can see how this writer worked hard to take what was given and run with it, so to speak. She continued:

Seconds later, two male hikers trudged into the clearing, and sank thankfully onto the dewy picnic bench.

Here is a different solution:

The only noise was the birds and the wind. No human signs were here other than the two picnic tables. Almost silently, a lean man strutted out of the forest, as if he was friends with the birds, and sat down on the table that was thawing in the morning sunlight.

This approach is more about mood. For now I ignore "as if he was," which should be "as if he were." The transition from the first paragraph is more perfunctory, but still, the writer has continued from the given setting. He then continues with the character:

He was a tall, middle-aged man, with long, almost black hair and tanned skin. He walked barefoot, and his feet showed the scars of living in the wilderness. His tattered shorts and tank top were all he wore and he only carried a small backpack with his living necessities.

Our writer has not penetrated the picture vividly enough to avoid having the man wearing only a tank top while the picnic table is still thawing. Nor am I convinced by the bare feet and wilderness. However, the next sentence tells us what the "living necessities" were and why the man was at the pond.

The bag contained a knife, a water bottle that he topped off when he reached water, a blanket, and a fire kit. He set down his bag and removed his top showing his strong sunburned back. He then dove into the pond, scaring the birds *[a good reference back to the first paragraph]* and swam in the clear water. His tired face became rejuvenated in the chilling pool, showing his brilliant green eyes.

My comment on the writer's paper: You wouldn't have seen the color of his eyes when he was in the pool. That sentence was then scratched out. The picture ends like this:

After getting refreshed in the cold water, the man climbed out, unrolled the blanket on the table *[again, a good reference to the beginning paragraph]*, and lay down to rest.

Actually, our writer wrote: "…and layed down to rest." This is perhaps one of the most frequent grammatical errors. More on that in our "Lie/Lay" section, page 103.

And for a third variation from an 8th grader who found the notion of "picture" hard to grasp, as she was far more interested in facts and information; a child who was "imagination poor"[12] but really eager to understand my instructions:

Piercing through, the autumn sun shone down onto this park. It was so awake and alive with all the wildlife swimming in the shimmering pond and flittering through the tree tops. Unexpectedly, the sound of footsteps were *[sic]* heard, trampling through the reeds on the edge of the pond, which started all the birds screeching and flapping. A tall thin man with a box stumbled out, almost falling into the murky water. He was a bird watcher, no more than thirty years old. As he finally caught his balance, he opened his box excitedly and pulled out a fancy pair of binoculars. He held the black binoculars up to his chocolate brown eyes, which matched his hair, and took a glance around the land. As he was scanning, he stopped with a jerk. Sitting still at the top of a maple tree, was the bird he had been looking for all his life. He didn't know what it was called, but had seen many pictures. After a minute or two, the bird flew off and out of sight. The bird watcher packed up, stumbled back into the reeds, heading to his car. He went home extremely happy, for this small wonder made his day.

Finally, a bit of a self-portrait.

Sitting at the base of a tree was a teenage girl. Her strawberry-blonde hair framed her fair face and her green eyes scanned the calculus book in her lap. The gentle breeze picked up and blew her hair across her face in all directions. As she tried to keep her hair under control the wind licked through her book and she lost her page. Exasperated she pulled her hair into a knot, picked up her book and stalked out of the park. Maybe she could find a quiet, cozy, coffee shop to do her math. After squeezing by crowds on crosswalk and slipping through crowded sidewalks she arrived at her go-to corner: Kelly's Coffee. She opened the door and the hot, sweet smell hit her like opening an oven full of baking cookies. All the tables were taken in the tiny shop, so she decided to share a booth with… *[out of time]*

We tried this again with different settings which were so specific that providing character and plot became a tempting puzzle, instead of an onerous task.

Sea weed, shells and bits of straw outlined the high water line along the beach. Great boulders rose out of the shallows. Just where the tide surged around them, starfish clung to the exposed rock. Sea gulls wheeled above. From among the bull rushes in the nearby tidal marsh, red-winged blackbirds called out.

or:

Tumbleweed clung to the barbed wire as the wind surged across the dunes. Flying sand blotted out the sky. Along the fence line, straggling cotton trees bent under the onslaught. Intermittent silence interrupted the steady roar.

This method of providing the beginning of a story and asking the students to continue to write on can be channeled toward other specific tasks. For example, here is the beginning of a description, where the task was to focus on the characters. The students had to finish the story.

Harriet was in the habit of scanning her customers while she scanned their groceries in the checkout line. She'd been working at the store for three months. Twice a week after school and on Saturday afternoons she stood and picked pre-packaged food, frankfurters, shrink-wrapped cheese, and cartons of frozen food off the conveyor belt. Always there was another customer and then one after that. It was tiring work. And it was relentless and after a while she felt herself going into a daze. That was how the troubles started.

Harriet was biding her time, making money at this job, so she could attend veterinary school in the city. She had always loved animals, and had nursed various feathered fledglings, kittens and even injured snakes back to health. She was known in the neighborhood as a reliable dog and cat sitter. She dreamed of owning a horse. Her parents had plenty of money, but they did not support her dream of veterinary school. They felt it was beneath their daughter's station in life to cure animals. She ought to be a doctor, they said. "You can go to vet school, but we won't pay a penny," they had told her.

She was a junior in high school, and she kept up with her schoolwork, took care of the animals, and then she had this tedious job.

She was mindlessly scanning groceries, and as was her habit now, she looked up at the next customer, and woke up right away.

Given such a running start, even the reluctant writers bounce onward with the story. For a class boasting at least half a dozen ambitious ballerinas, I modified Harriet's dream:

Harriet was in the habit of scanning her customers while she scanned their groceries in the checkout line. She'd been working at the store for three months. Twice a week after school and on Saturday afternoons she stood and picked pre-packaged food, frankfurters, shrink-wrapped cheese, and cartons of frozen food off the conveyor belt. Always there was another customer and then one after that. It was tiring work. And it was relentless and after a while she felt herself going into a daze. That was how the troubles started.

Harriet was biding her time, making money at this job, so she could attend ballet school in the city. She had the delicate build of a dancer, and the sort of face that would not stand out on the stage. She would blend in, like the carefully chosen wallpaper in her parents' home. Her parents had plenty of money, but they did not support her dream of ballet. "You can go to ballet school, but we won't pay a penny," they had told her.

She was a sophomore in high school, and she kept up with her schoolwork, but she practiced at the ballet studio every day and then she had this tedious job.

She was mindlessly scanning groceries, and as was her habit now, she looked up at the next customer, and woke up right away. It was her father.

On the basis of the students' continuations, I can introduce the "conflict" part of story writing. Who is that next customer? Why does the writer introduce him or her? What short exchange of dialogue provides us with enough clues to understand why we are bothering to mention the encounter? How does the encounter end?

Or I might provide a character, characterized according to the methods we've worked on, and ask the students to continue the story, i.e., the plot with its turning point.

In the final seconds of the game, the tallest of the basketball players scored a shot from the free-throw line. His sky-blue shorts and vest flopped around his skinny knees and elbow. Whenever he tossed the ball, he also tossed his long, blond mop of hair. Most engaging was his unexpected smile, which flashed on his freckled face every time he was pleased with himself.

Do we see that, by describing the actions, we've also characterized the basketball player? He is athletic, and by the sound of it, popular and self-confident.

What can we tell about this fisherman from the clues the writer (in this case, the teacher) has provided?

Knee deep in the swiftly flowing river, the angler patiently waited, both hands on his fishing rod. As protection from the sun, he wore a broad-brimmed, white hat, which had seen better days. Green, waterproof pants and bib rose to his shoulders. The nozzle of a hydration pack was stuck through his suspenders. The tip of his rod started to bend, and the fisherman awoke, like a statue coming to life.

The older the students, the more likely they are to grasp the concept of indirect characterization, i.e., telling the reader about the personality or circumstances of the character by describing the telling details. Which words in the description of the fisherman are clues?

Subordinating Conjunctions:
"When in disgrace with fortune and men's eyes…"

In our consideration of transitions up to this point, we've worked with the idea of taking a detail of the given picture to develop the picture further. We expand our view logically, organically. A different way of linking sentences is through the judicious use of subordinating conjunctions:

after	just in case
although	now that once
as	only if
as soon as	since
because	the first time
before	though
by the time	unless
even if	until

even though	when
every time	whenever
if	whereas
in case	whether or not
in the event that	while

Grammatically, subordinating conjunctions bridge two different types of clauses. The subordinating conjunction is the first word in a subordinate (or dependent) clause. For our purposes, what's important is not so much the grammar—although the grammar affects the punctuation and therefore must be learned along the way—but the coherent, logical way these subordinating conjunctions relate two parts of a sentence. Whenever a subordinating conjunction is used, the two aspects of the sentence are organized. Their relationship becomes clear.

Because subordinating conjunctions succinctly relate two thoughts to each other, they provide flow and direction to our writing. Grammatically, a sentence with a subordinating conjunction is a complex sentence. When students use them, their writing becomes more sophisticated. Students should be encouraged to use them—in moderation.

As an exercise, we might provide a short list of these subordinating conjunctions and then ask the students to fill in the blanks. Grammatically, any of the given words will do. However, the meaning of the sentence will change according to our choice, and we should be able to defend that choice.

while	until
because	although
since	

1. _____ of the bad weather, the class hike was canceled.
2. I didn't really mind, _____ I usually enjoy our hikes.
3. _____ our teacher was unprepared to teach, we got to play games indoors.
4. _____ he went to get board games, we moved the furniture to the edges of the room.
5. We enjoyed ourselves with various mild forms of entertainment _____ the end of the day. On the whole, I prefer hiking.

Or you could find some great examples and ask the students to complete the sentence:

When in disgrace with fortune and men's eyes,
I all alone beweep my outcast state…

> – Shakespeare, Sonnet 29

Information vs. Picture

Below are examples of sentences written by students. I gave them the *informational* sentence; they had to come up with the *pictorial* sentence. Later they can do both. The writers here are the same ones quoted earlier: Aishe, Fionghoula, Sheryl, and Phineas

Information: Ralph was bored.

Picture:

1. Ralph sat at an empty table with nothing to do. *[Writer #1 added a parenthesis: "Gestures: yawning, tapping fingers, head in hand." This is a step forward for this writer, who now needs to learn how to bring these parenthetical gestures into the main sentence.]* (A)
2. Ralph's expression appeared blank and bored. *["Appeared" is on the Avoid List.]* (F)
3. Ralph sat on his chair in class, staring into space. (S)
4. Ralph's tired eyes stared off, totally unaware of the lesson. (P)

Information: It was early morning in the town.

Picture:

1. Peeking over the church, the sun slowly rose up. *[We try to avoid personification, as it is usually unwarranted. So "peeking" is not really allowed. Furthermore, the sun rises quickly when measured against something along the eastern horizon.]* (A)
2. The sun had barely begun to shine over the tall buildings. *[This doesn't actually make sense.]* (F)

3. Birds chirped and flitted above roof tops through the crisp morning air. (S)
4. The first light of day reflected off the shop windows. (P)

Information: Because of the weather, Miss Winter was cold.

Picture:

1. Miss Winter shivered in the brisk air. (A)
2. Because of the unmelting frost on the ground, Miss Winter felt chilly. *[F. is an excellent writer—technically. Hence she is used to getting good marks for her writing. For her 8th grade project, this student wrote a novel. Clearly she identifies with being a good writer. But her pictures are unpenetrated. She is fluent, and her words flow easily. Her spelling and punctuation are more reliable than mine, but she doesn't really dig into the meaning of what she is saying. And where did this excellent student find "unmelting"?!]* (F)
3. The freezing air chilled Miss Winter to the bone. *[Is this really more pictorial, or has writer R gotten tired?]* (S)
4. Miss Winter shivered in the chilling wind. (P)

A couple of days later, we tried another set of the same exercise, again as an in-class exercise.

Information: The school yard was crowded.

Picture:

1. Cheering first graders *[This student had written "Cheering children," then crossed out children and substituted "first graders"—much improved! Yeah!!]* shoved each other in order to get to the play structure *[but she didn't see that "play structure" could be a slide or swing].* (A)

2. In the dirty city playground, many laughing students milled around. (F)
3. Crowds tramped relentlessly about the shiny new school yard. *[Really?!]* (S)
4. Bustling with kindergartners, the school's small playground was loud and alive. *["Bustling" is nice, but "was" is a verb I discourage. By definition, it conveys information. This was a very good student who could be corrected without getting discouraged.]* (P)

Information: Many vegetables grew in the garden.

Picture :

1. High up in the sky, the sun shone on the rows of cherry tomatoes. *[She's trying, although the "high up in the sky" is unnecessary.]* (A)
2. Dozens of tomato plants wilted under the glare of the sun in the yard. (F)
3. The raised beds in the backyard were overflowing with squashes, carrots, celery, tomatoes and various lettuce. (S)
4. Ready for harvesting, the beets and carrots sat buried in the community garden. *[Nice! "Sat buried" isn't really personification, is it?]* (P)

Altogether better and better!

Information: He drove his car down the road.

Picture:

1. A teenage boy drove his pickup truck along the country road. (A)
2. A paramedic raced through the city in his flashing ambulance. (F)

3. As his limo raced from the paparazzi, Justin Bieber's driver lost control of the car and it skidded and flipped. (S)

4. Recklessly driven by Thomas, the recent college graduate, the '68 Chevy Nova blared down the lonely desert road. *[This sounds specific, but relies on names. Our good student could have done without those crutches.]* (P)

Our Information vs. Picture exercise reminds us of our first attempts to be specific. Now, however, we see that what we are after is imaginative clarity.

A Story in Four Paragraphs

Having learned to choose our words deliberately, to use the pictorial style of writing, vary our syntax, avoid the avoids, and understand the importance of transitions, it's time to write a story.

Turning Point

Surprisingly, the biggest challenge for writers, whether school-age or older, is to come up with a story in which something *happens.* This sounds almost comical, but it's not uncommon for novice writers to churn out pages of description, in which nothing really happens. There is no incident to anchor the story. The importance of a turning point has to be learned. In conventional writing classes, this turning point is sometimes called the "conflict," or more generally, "plot." I prefer "turning point."

A good way to introduce the concept of the turning point is to read a piece of writing without one and then ask, What happened? Well, nothing really happened. We had a beautiful description of an old mansion and its lovely estate, but nothing really happened.

A simple diagram can help:

The big loop represents a turning point. It is an incident in the story. Everything hinges on this moment in the story. There might be some smaller turning points before or after this big event, but what's important for the story is the big turning point. Usually the turning point comes in the second half of the story. It can even come at the very end. Sometimes it launches the story, as for example in much detective fiction. A short story classically relies on fewer such turning points, perhaps only one.

Our auxiliary reading can be helpful. What, for example, is the turning point in the short story about Young Jerry and the Yellow Dream Mine in "The Banks of the Sacramento" by Jack London? Well, there might be several turning points. Do we think one of them is the most dramatic and essential to the story?

Ideally, over the next few lessons, as we work on this concept of the turning point, we read aloud some short excerpts from published writing and diagram it for its turning points. Diagramming the drama of the story in this way appeals to those students who consider themselves scientists or mathematicians or athletes, rather than writers. It offers a concrete method, an objective analytic tool, and removes the onus of the "soft" literary realm.

Turning Point Exercises

We might now consider some scenarios for which we provide the turning point. If we were writing a story about something that happened on the way to school, for example, what sort of "incident" could we come up with? Let's make a list:

- run out of gas and…
- leave the house late and …
- forget your homework and …
- meet your friend on the way to school and …

Part of the task is to come up with an original incident, which although original is not fantastic. No, you cannot run into an elephant on the way to school. No, you can't have a car crash on the way to school. Yes, it could happen, but—thankfully—too unlikely. Here is a scale from likely to unlikely:

Unlikely   *Likely*

Where along this line would we put the elephant? The car crash? Leaving the house late?

Most of the time, students agree with one another on where along the scale to place the incident. Of course they will enjoy making up bizarre situations, but the greater challenge is to find something worth describing, something that is worth telling, something that has some drama in it, yet is not absurd, weird, fantastical…. Not as easy as it sounds. Your "imagination rich" children will rise to the task with unflagging inventiveness, whereas the "imagination poor"[13] will need a lot of practice to dig in.

I've rarely had pushback on the constraints I impose for this exercise, mostly because by now it's clear that we are building up a skill with precise parameters. However, if there were a furious demand to allow encountering an elephant on the way to school, I might, later on, prescribe a fairy tale or science fiction story. That would take some preparation to make it worthwhile. It's harder than it sounds. An original fairy tale is challenging, even for a 12th grader, even for adults.

So, using your most pictorial way of writing, describe how you got to school this morning, BUT: include an "incident" that you make up to fit the setting. Remember: nothing weird, fantastic, or bizarre. You have to describe something that actually *could* happen, yet is out of the ordinary enough to warrant description. Describing your mom stopping the car at a stop sign is not story material. We need a relevant turning point, one which is innately connected to driving to school.

It will take several lessons to build up the notion of "incident." We can provide subsequent in-class and homework exercises to practice our understanding of a relevant, possible, interesting incident.

Our "Something Happened on the Way to School This Morning" story will benefit from an outline. It's the same sequence we used way back when we passed our papers to our neighbors. It's the same sequence we've used in our sentence stories.

Paragraph 1: Setting
Paragraph 2: Character
Paragraph 3: What happens. The Incident or Turning Point
Paragraph 4: Resolution or Conclusion

Having worked with this notion of the turning point, we are now ready to write an entirely original story in which the writer invents the turning point. However, providing guidelines is still advisable. A good entry point for this first story is to take the setting from a previous exercise, for example, the Beach or the Forest we worked on earlier, and to use that as the basis.

Now we can hearken back to our earlier exercise, where we had one sentence for each of these topics. This time, we'll have a paragraph instead of a sentence for each part. Again we'll use our trusty outline.

1: Setting
2: Character
3: What happens. The Incident or Turning Point
4: Resolution or Conclusion

Of course we have to make use of the other tools we've been honing: specific vocabulary, transitions.

This is the first complete, original story. We've labored on getting the ingredients ready, now it's time to cook. A big deal ought to be made of this moment.

Reading Each Other's Stories to Find the Turning Point

Youngsters love to hear each other's work, as their own comments attest (see "What Did You Enjoy Most in This Course?" page 176). My preferred method is to read two or three examples of the corrected homework I'm about to return. Having a "workshop atmosphere" in which we learn from each other is instructive in many ways. We discover that a sparkling sentence or captivating word choice can occur where we don't expect it; we gain surprising insights about each other; self-knowledge is promoted when we hear our classmates' solutions to the assignment. As long as the teacher maintains an atmosphere of objectivity and practices tact with her commentary, so that the weak students can shine and the strong students can find ways to improve their work, these sessions of sharing the homework provide an enjoyable social lubricant as well as a level playing field regardless of talent. Talent easily misses the point of the assignment.

Fundamental Principle Number Three:
If a student writes on his or her paper "Don't read this aloud,"
I don't mention the writer's name. In general, however, I promote
a "workshop atmosphere" by attributing authorship.

Although there are students who can read their own work aloud without flinching, mumbling or over-dramatizing, I like to read the students' work aloud myself. That way I can insert an editorial reflection, point out a particularly successful turn of phrase, or ask a pertinent question to clarify or suggest an alternative where needed. Students who struggle to express themselves in writing can be encouraged and motivated when the teacher finds even one detail to praise aloud before the whole class.

It's important that the teacher knows which papers will be read aloud. They need to have been selected deliberately, for their different purposes.

"See whether you can find a strikingly apt word," is a useful guide for listening. Adults too will be startled by how often there is agreement about that one perfect word.

Once these first stories have been corrected, and you've had a chance to read some of them to the class, you will find the need to talk about the pitfalls of mere convenience in a story.

Convenience

Now this word *convenient* carries a very useful concept. If your story is about a hiker on a steep mountain side, it's merely convenient if, as he wearily approaches the summit, his Russell terrier's collar breaks—unless the writer has introduced the dog earlier in the journey. A story requires a structure that can carry it. We can't just plop a femur onto a collar bone. If a particular object, such as the terrier's collar, becomes crucial to the story, we have to find a way to introduce it earlier. Otherwise, it is merely convenient. That is why *rewriting* is an essential component of writing. That is why it is beneficial to work through several drafts of the story.

The younger the students, the more difficult it is for them to change their own work for the sake of improving the story, its flow, the structure, or any of its details. The older the students, the more likely they are to be able to appreciate the need for "kneading" the story, until there are no air bubbles left. Only then is it ready to be baked, i.e., made public. Of course when we are working through exercises or first drafts, we are not looking to go public; we are still promoting a workshop atmosphere. But it would be a wonderful goal in a high school class, for instance, to produce a collection of short stories or, at the very least, include some of them in a literary magazine, or blog, or the school's newsletter.

12 Rule Number Twelve:
Good writing should never resort to mere convenience.

Exercise to Avoid Mere Convenience

A quick in-class exercise, which can be done orally with the class as a whole, is to agree on a suggestive object, say, a life vest or a concert ticket or a key.... No, not a key, it will just lead to a clichéd lost key. Ask the students to jot down an outline of how this object first appears in the story and then appears later on as a crucial device.

A. Life vest
1. Family goes boating.
2. Dad insists that everyone wears life vests.
3. Stormy weather comes.
4. Difficult to moor the boat
5. Must wait out the storm in the harbor
6. Everyone glad to have life vest

or:

B. Concert ticket
1. Ordered online
2. Printed at home
3. Placed in pocket of concert-going pants
4. On day of concert, other pants worn
5. At ticket gate, disaster strikes.

Or: matches, wedding ring, cell phone…. Any object can serve the purpose, though some are more instantly provocative.

The main thing here is to introduce a prop which turns out to be crucial later. It's a basic idea, with a long reach, because it helps to make the story organic and inherently logical. It strengthens the fabric of the story. Again, the students' tendency will be to come up with extremes, such as jackknives or rabid wolves, but we'll veto those suggestions.

To construct such stories, in which the details are interconnected and the transitions tight, an active imagination is necessary. For 7th and especially for 8th graders and beyond, this is a revelation. Good writers emerge through these exercises in logic and precision. Florid sentences are no longer enough. Suddenly, unexpectedly, a quiet boy excels in a subject he's never taken much interest in before. What we are really doing here is working on the carefully controlled content of the "Thinking Exercise."[14] But we cannot be merely logical. Our stories must also have heart. That's the part that usually pulses healthily, when the scaffold is secure. The more precise the words, the more compelling the pictures and thus the story will be, and the more heart and breath the story will have. I wouldn't talk this way to the youngsters, but it's good for the teacher to realize this, and, of course, adult students can work consciously with such an idea.

Below is a composition in which an object plays a major role. This is a revised draft, and I've corrected the spelling and punctuation errors that remained.

See a Penny

Kyle Turner looked up in excitement. All above him were lights, colors, and machines of large proportions. Ferris wheels, zippers and slides all the way down to small booths where you could have your picture taken. Kyle stared in awe, only roused from his reverie by his mother tugging him out of the way of an elderly couple.

Kyle followed his mother through one of the lanes lined by game booths and food stands. Along the way his senses were overpowered by the screaming children, fluorescent stuffed prizes and the overwhelming stench of oil and sugar.

As he was walking along, Kyle noticed a gleam out of the corner of his eye. He broke free from his mother's grip and went over to investigate. Upon further inspection Kyle realized it was a penny. He picked it up as his mother caught up with him. "See a penny, pick it up, and all the day you'll have good luck," his mother said. Kyle smiled but then looked more serious. "If I drop it, will I have bad luck?" he asked. "That's what they say," said his mother.

Over the next two hours Kyle did indeed have good luck. At one game he threw a ring on a bottle and won a giant blue and white panda. At another, a lucky shot into a hoop earned him a beach ball. Even the lady at the Ferris wheel said he could ride for free because he was "so cute."

After getting off the Ferris wheel, Kyle was running to the cotton candy stand when he tripped. The penny which he had been holding fell from his grip. Remembering his mother's words from earlier he stared in horror at the little piece of copper as it tinkled against the pavement. He quickly reached down and snapped it off the pavement trying to pretend that nothing had happened.

Half an hour later the boy was still wary but was trying to enjoy himself. He was running to get in line for a ride when he slipped on a rock. The ground rushed to meet him and he was helpless. His knees scraped against the pavement. He howled and clutched them as blood began to trickle down his calves. Rushing over to his side, his mother tried to comfort him. "Last time I ever pick up a penny," he thought as they hobbled home.

The writer is now a junior in college. In response to my request for any thoughts or memories about our 8th grade block, he sent me the following:

> I remember that class in 8th grade because it was one of the few times in middle school when I was told, "Good job, but do it again." There was a real emphasis on doing things differently and improving.

Why Active Voice?

By the time they've reached 8th grade, most students have learned the difference between active and passive voice. Knowing the difference between these two voices is helpful. Although there are circumstances when using the passive voice is essential, for our purposes, learning to use crisp, engaging, pictorial language, active voice is preferable.

Just to be sure we're all on the same page about this, I generally review these two voices by way of the standard exercise of turning the one into the other.

> Jeremy completed his homework.
> The homework was completed by Jeremy.

> In the hurricane, the eucalyptus on the hill was blown down.
> The hurricane blew down the eucalyptus at the top of the hill.

In the second example, there's a good reason to use passive voice, because the tree is what we're describing. In the first sentence, we're pointing out that Jeremy completed his homework, so he has to be active. It requires some subtlety of thought to understand the difference, but I'm assuming that the fundamentals were covered in 5th grade. Now, in 8th and beyond, we might ponder the difference in emphasis between:

The baker kneaded the dough.
The dough was kneaded by the baker.

or:

Three drops of Biuret were added to the test tube.
Our teacher added the Biuret to the test tube.

Quite a lively conversation might be had by the students.

The point is, there's nothing wrong with passive voice. However, active voice will make for more active writing, and that's what we're after. If we really need to say that something was on the receiving end of an action, then, certainly, passive is the way to get that across.

Whether we use active or passive might be a matter of emphasis. Below are some examples in which the emphasis on the object, rather than on the action, dictates passive voice:

How *is* his name *pronounced*?
That house *has been being watched* for weeks.
I saw it *being eaten* by the cat.[15]

These examples come from a sophisticated chart on the internet, providing excellent examples in all tenses. Here is a succinct explanation:

Passive voice is used when the action is the focus, not the subject. It is not important (or not known) who does the action.
- The window is broken. (It is not known who broke the window, or it is not important to know who broke the window.)

- The class has been canceled. (The focus is on the class being canceled. It is not important to know who canceled it.)
- The passive voice is often used. (The focus is on the passive voice. It is not important to explain who the writer is.)[16]

This is a good point. We can legitimately use passive voice when it's not important to know who did it. But the very same source then continues with:

> Passive voice should be avoided when you want more clarity in writing.

Exactly. That's the point here. So in general, we should avoid passive voice, because when it's used gratuitously, it vitiates the writing we are striving so hard to activate. After all, we know how important the verb is—it is the king of the sentence and rules the subject. So we should promote that verb, not dim it down. Let's add this to our Avoid List, and let's add this new Rule:

13 *Rule Number Thirteen: Use active voice whenever possible.*

Then, too, let's define *active* and *passive* and provide some examples in our grammar section.

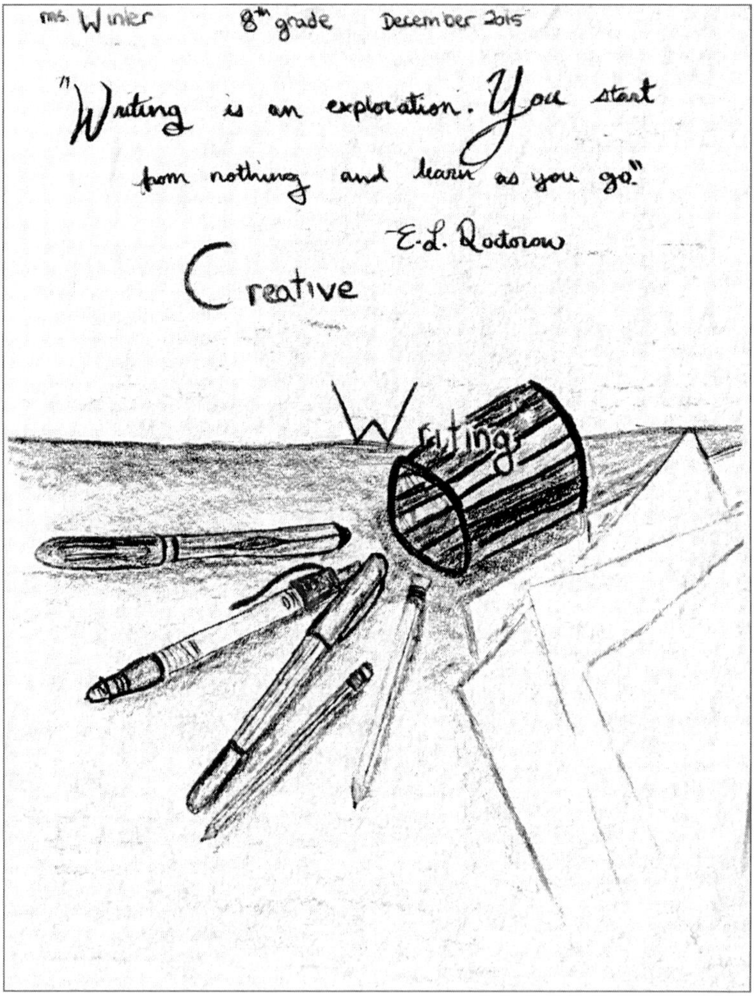
ms. Winler
8th grade
December 2015
"Writing is an exploration. You start from nothing and learn as you go."
-E.L. Doctorow
Creative
Writing

The Eternal Review of Some Grammar Basics

English is plagued by homonyms. As common as flours, they pray on the board, the week, the deer and the fare. Of course, the plethora of same-sounding/different-meaning words is why we sometimes just can't bare one more wine of the homonym punsters. Enough, enough!

For our purposes, we'll focus on just four. We could eliminate 82% (unofficial statistic) of all spelling errors if we could just get these four sorted out, and that's true for adults as well as children at all levels of their education. I call these four "Confusing Words," and I invent drills, oral and written, with many variations, so that after a while we can use these pesky words with the routine of a familiar times-table.

Confusing Words: *its, there, too, were*

Why is it that so many students reach 8th grade and are still confused about these words? It's not because they haven't heard about them! No, it's the great homonym maw awaiting the dreamy, the heedless, the sloppy. You have to think about whether it's *its* or *it's*. First of all, of course, I explain it all over again. We put the rules in the Rules section of our binder.

its = possessive   it's = it is   etc.

Then, for the next four or five days, we practice various drills as part of our warm-up. We build up our its-it's-there-they're-their-to-too-were-we're-where muscles. The most obvious exercise would look something like this:

Exercise for Confusing Words

Directions: Fill in either *its* or *Its* or *it's* or *It's*.

1. _____ 8:15; where are the students?
2. _____ no use complaining.
3. This pen has lost _____ cap.
4. The school and _____ grounds were groomed for the visitors.
5. The class was on _____ best behavior during the 2nd grade play.
6. I don't know where it is. _____ not here.
7. This is a lettuce. _____ Latin name is *Lactuca sativa.*
8. The pencil has lost _____ eraser.
9. I'm looking up _____ spelling in the dictionary.
10. _____ a nuisance having to think through every *its* and *it's*.

If you don't remind the students about capitalizing the first word of the sentence, they will forget, which will mean no credit. If you are looking to challenge your grammar leaders, don't remind them about capitalization.

The next step is to dictate sentences. That's harder.

When we feel more comfortable with both the written and oral versions of this, meaning, once we begin to think through our choice before writing it down, we can go to yet another variation. We ask the students to make up a paragraph using as many sentences as possible with *its/it's/Its* or *It's*. Better yet, we ask the students to make up the paragraph but leave blank spaces for the *its/it's/Its* or *It's*. Then we have the students exchange papers. Then the one who made up the sentences gets to correct the one who filled in the blanks. This quiz then goes into the "In Class" section of our binders. Sometimes, I ask in a general sort of way, "Who got them all right?" "Who got 1 to 3 wrong?" and so forth. This gives me and everyone else a sense of how we're doing.

Once I sense that almost all of us have mastered these little troublemakers, it becomes a S10X (sentence ten times) word. That means that if I find it used incorrectly, the entire sentence, or at a minimum the phrase in which it's used, must be written out ten times with the troublemaker underlined each time. This may seem draconian, but we have to resort to strong measures to tame the little monster.

Now we can use the same sequence of exercises and drills on the others: *there, too* and *were* (even though *were* and *we're* and *where* are not, strictly speaking, homonyms, they pose a challenge because they are easily confused, so I include them in this set.). Finally, we can use all four in the same exercise. Then we might find a paragraph that looks like this (example by a student):

_____ are _____ many things _____ _____ today. I could _____ this or I could _____ that. But _____ is that shirt I wanted to _____. _____ there, but _____ dirty and _____ collar is crinkled. I could _____ that _____, but I'm going to my friend's house and _____, at their house, I must look good.

There are too many things to wear today. I could wear this or I could wear that. But there is that shirt I wanted to wear. It's there, but it's dirty and its collar is crinkled. I could wear that too, but I'm going to my friend's house and there, at their house, I must look good.

Or it might sound like this (also the result of the homework assignment to come up with a paragraph shot through with our confusing words, leaving blanks to be filled in by a classmate). Needless to say, the challenge of challenging classmates is a successful incentive.

Theodore walked to the room _____ the _____boys _____ seated. "I don't know if _____ supposed _____ bring cookies _____ or if _____ bringing all we need _____," he said. "What are we supposed_____ _____?" asked Billy. "Whatever _____ gonna be, _____ got _____ have _____ buttons," replied Frank. "Oh no! Don't tell me we don't even know _____ _____ supposed _____ go or whether we need _____ bring something _____!" said Theodore. "_____ getting _____ be_____ late," said Billy. "So let's just go_____ _____ _____ house is, and let's bring Joe, the dog _____." Then Theodore and the_____ other boys left _____ go _____ the party and they _____ excited _____.

Clearly, this writer enjoyed the task. We discover, in filling in the blanks, that sometimes more than one answer is possible. My favorite:

Theodore walked to the room where the two boys were seated. "I don't know if we're supposed to bring cookies too or if they're bringing all we need there," he said. "What are we supposed to wear?" asked Billy. "Whatever it's gonna be, it's got to have two buttons," replied Frank. "Oh no! Don't tell me we don't even know where we're supposed to go or whether we need to bring something too!" said Theodore. "It's getting to be too late," said Billy. "So let's just go to where their house is, and let's bring Joe, the dog, too." Then Theodore and the two other boys left to go to the party, and they were excited, too.

In making up the written quiz or exercise, I like to use sentences that relate to the class. For example:

Fill in the blanks using *their*, *there* or *they're.*

1. Most of the time, the 8th graders have _____ homework.
2. Sometimes, though, _____very sleepy when they arrive.
3. It makes you wonder what _____ parents are doing about bedtime.
4. Often _____ is a student who arrives during the verse.
5. When that happens, it would be best if they waited _____, by the door.
6. _____ excuses often have something to do with their automobile.
7. Is _____ anything we can do about it?
8. I'll have to talk to _____ parents.
9. On the whole _____ a hard-working group.
10. _____ over _____ with _____ classmates.

Two Especially Confusing Words: lie *and* lay

During the 25 or so years that I read the hundreds of stories, compositions and essays by adult students, I observed that *lie* and *lay* flummoxed even good, literate, educated writers. It's no wonder then, that this triplet of tripper-uppers (yes, there are three bothersome confusers) trips up even erudite younger students.

> *lie,* noun: a false statement made with deliberate intent to deceive; an intentional untruth; a falsehood
> *to lie,* verb: to speak falsely or utter untruth knowingly, as with intent to deceive
> "To lie," when an untruth is involved, is a regular verb:
>   I lie today, I will lie tomorrow, I lied yesterday.

The real confusion is *lie* as in "lie down," and *lay,* as when you place an object.

> The first:
> *to lie,* verb: to be, or place oneself, at rest in a flat, horizontal, or recumbent position; recline (intransitive verb – i.e., the verb can't have a direct object).

> The second:
> *to lay,* verb: to put or place in a horizontal position or position of rest; set down: to lay a book on a desk (transitive verb – it must have an object).

Experts agree: *lay* and *lie* have been tripping up English speakers for 700 years, and no one should be judged harshly for being among the confused. The pair is a doozy.[17] Here is a wonderfully succinct explanation I found online:

Lay **or** *Lie?*

Lay means "to place something down." It is something you do to **something else.** It is a transitive verb.

Incorrect: Lie the book on the table.

Correct: Lay the book on the table. (It is being done to something else.)

Lie means "to recline" or "be placed." It does **not** act on anything or anyone else. It is an intransitive verb.

Incorrect: Lay down on the couch.

Correct: Lie down on the couch. (It is not being done to anything else.)

The reason **lay** and **lie** are confusing is their **past tenses.**

The past tense of **lay** is **laid.**

The past tense of **lie** is **lay.**

Incorrect: I lay it down here yesterday.

Correct: I laid it down here yesterday. (It is being done to something else.)

Incorrect: Last night I laid awake in bed.

Correct: Last night I lay awake in bed. (It is not being done to anything else.)

The **past participle** of **lie** is **lain.** The **past participle** of **lay** is like the past tense, **laid.**

Examples: I could have lain in bed all day.

They have laid an average of 500 feet of sewer line a day.

Layed is a misspelling and does not exist. Use **laid.**[18]

What's more, both *lie* and *lay* are used idiomatically to mean a great many different things, including sexual intercourse. For upper grades students, such idioms, proverbs and sayings thus constitute an entirely different level of study.

Apart from all these commonly confused words—*its, there, too, where,* and *lie/lied/lay/laid*—there is another widespread and annoyingly persistent pair of grammar grotesques: the sentence fragment and the run-on sentence. I find these culprits harder to clean up than the confusing words.

Sentence Fragments and Run-On Sentences

To subdue them, we need a sense for the sentence, which really should start in 3rd grade. Because these fragment/run-on jokers were already cartwheeling through students' written work when I started teaching over four decades ago, I know that sentence mayhem didn't just erupt out of the corruption of language brought on by texting and other media idiosyncrasies. These sentence invalids—masquerading as authentic, legitimate sentences, but actually being just feeble and incomplete or witlessly burbling along with no regard to form—are stubborn.

I think that to wrestle these unruly non-sentences to the mat, a teacher needs at least an equal measure of stubbornness, a surfeit of will. If the fragment and the run-on are extirpated early in the students' schooling, all the better. But if we encounter them in 7th and 8th grades and beyond, as we do, then we need to work with the students who still don't get it and patiently devise as many exercises and drills as it takes. We'll have to go back to the subject-predicate foundation of the sentence. A lot can be done through the ear. Can we teach the students to hear the difference between a formally correct sentence and the kind that is either not complete, or really more than one sentence?

Students who suffer from the fragment/run-on syndrome generally don't like to stop and think. They're used to having someone else do that for them. These are generally the students who are geniuses at slipping through any net you devise for them, and once they understand that this is one net they cannot escape, they will often improve fast. Once there are consequences, possibly very inconvenient consequences, for using sentence fragments or omitting the punctuation and capitalization needed to cure a run-on sentence, the students become their own physicians. Very often the problem has been that they were able to get away with sentence scrambles. Once we're on a campaign to root out this problem, and we persist with tenacious stubbornness (or have a special tutor for no other purpose), the worst offenders can make great progress.

When I encounter these non-sentence offenders, I sentence the offending writer to the boring task of rewriting the run-on correctly at least three times. It has to be neat and legible. If I can anticipate that this student won't know how to correct the problem, I correct it. Otherwise, I expect the student to figure it out. Ditto with the fragments.

Making the student answerable is the first step. We have to up the ante. We have to force the issue. I've taught plenty of youngsters who've been consigned to the remedial corner who would benefit greatly from a truly persistent teacher.

Again, a basic and effective method is to work one concept through thoroughly before moving on. Axiomatic though such an approach is, it's hard to apply because of the great range of rates at which students "get" what we're teaching. Our issue will be with the ones who are slow to grasp, and slower to apply. But the truly therapeutic attitude will have "the courage to teach," to paraphrase a slogan from the medical world.[19]

To master the sentence, we first have to recognize what constitutes a sentence. Then we can go on to work with the sentence-pretenders.

Fundamental Principle Number Four:

Take time to build up the basics with practice and more practice, until some measure of competence and reliability is reached, before moving on to the subtler or more complex aspects of the problem.

And yet, there is a realm where sentence fragments are legit: dialogue. Students enjoy working with dialogue. They like to include it in their stories. They like to get up in front of their peers and perform the dialogues they've written.

Dialogue and Quotation Marks

Quotation marks have to be explained again and again. Luckily, students love to use them in their stories. They feel as if they are writing a real story when they include dialogue. I stave off the use of dialogue until we have mastered the basics. Dialogue often becomes a red herring, a distraction, causing the students to lose track of the actual task in the assignment. So as we enter the last quarter of our block, we review the rules for quotation marks.

I found quite a few useful explanations and exercises online. The main thing to understand is the punctuation that the use of quotation marks requires. Does the final period go inside the quotation marks? Yes, it does, and when I find the universal hedge, which looks like a semicolon, I mark it as wrong. I warn the students that the punctuation must always be unmistakably clear.

Interrupted quotation marks are even more complicated than straightforward quotes because they change the punctuation rules. We have to know whether the second part of the quotation is a continuation of the phrase which comes before the interruption, or not.

Here is something straight off the internet, which can help set the teacher straight.

INTERRUPTED (OR DIVIDED) QUOTATION
Sometimes a writer needs to interrupt or divide a quotation. In interrupted quotations, the *speaker tag* comes in the middle of the quotation and in the middle of the sentence. The *speaker tag* is the part of the sentence that tells the reader who is talking.

Examples of speaker tags:
    he said
    the boy stated
    exclaimed Mary
    the teacher explained
    asked Bill

First, let us look at some regular quotations with speaker tags. Here is a regular quotation with the speaker tag at the beginning of the quoted sentence:
My brother said, "I need the car today, so I can go to work."
Here is another regular quotation with the speaker tag at the end of the quoted sentence:
"When you do your math homework tonight, remember to show all of your work," explained the teacher.

We can make both of these sentences into interrupted quotations by putting the speaker tag in the middle of the quoted sentence:

"I need the car today," <u>my brother said</u>, "so I can go to work."

"When you do your math homework tonight," <u>explained the teacher</u>, "remember to show all of your work."

Rules for writing interrupted quotations:

1. Use quotation marks around both parts of the interrupted quotation.

Examples:

"The book," whispered the librarian, "is on the second shelf by the wall."

"When Mom comes home," my sister said, "tell her I'm going to Sandy's house."

2. Quotations are separated from the speaker tag with commas.

A) For the first half of the quotation, put the comma inside the quotation marks.

B) For the second half of the quotation, put the comma after the speaker tag.

Examples:

"Did you know," asked the teacher, "that salamanders are amphibians?"

Notice that the first comma is after the word "know" and inside the quotation marks.

The second comma is after the word "teacher" and before the second set of quotation marks.

"My love," swooned the man, "will you marry me?"

Notice that the first comma is after the word "love" and inside the quotation marks.

The second comma is after the word "man" and before the second set of quotation marks.

3. Follow normal capitalization rules.
A) Capitalize the first word in the sentence.
Examples:
"Your dog ran out the door," she said, "because you left it open."
"My husband took me out for my birthday," Mrs. Smith exclaimed, "and then gave me new earrings!"
B) The second half of the quotation does not begin with a capital letter, unless it is a proper noun or title.
Examples:
"Please tell your parents," the man on the phone said, "Amy will be there at 5:00."
In this sentence, "Amy" is capitalized in the second half of the quotation because it is a name and a proper noun.
"Students," Miss Smith instructed, "please line up at the door."
In this sentence, "please" is not capitalized because it is not a proper noun or a title.
"Miss Smith" is capitalized because it is a proper noun.

4. End punctuation goes inside the final quotation marks
Incorrect:
"Did you know," asked Mrs. Jones, "that the sunflower is the state flower of Kansas"?
Correct:
"Did you know," asked Mrs. Jones, "that the sunflower is the state flower of Kansas?"
Incorrect:
"When your brother gets home," my dad yelled, "tell him I need to talk to him in my office"!

Correct:
"When your brother gets home," my dad yelled, "tell him I
need to talk to him in my office!"

Helpful as these indications can be for the teacher, they need
to be broken down into smaller chunks to be palatable for the
students—and I've found that to be true for students of any age.

It can be helpful to begin the quotation mark campaign by having
the students become playwrights of sorts. They can work together in
small groups to come up with a dialogue.

Providing a scenario, that is, providing the situation in which the
dialogue takes place, yields the best results. For one thing, we can
enjoy each other's dramatizations all the more when we've all had
the same challenge. For another, being given the situation eliminates
the need to come up with one. And, if the teacher is the one to
decide who is talking and why, we are less likely to find ourselves
stalled in a brackish backwater trying to think up a scenario. One of
my favorite scenarios involves a mother and a son at the department
store, looking for pants that the son is to wear at his uncle's wedding.

The last class of 8th graders attempting this came up with
hilarious results, in which they brilliantly mocked their own
penchant for avoiding formal dress. The skits were worthy of
performance, and I was sorry that I hadn't anticipated a production,
at least for the 6th and 7th grades and any other teachers.

If we introduce spoken words in a story by actually hearing
dialogue spoken, the bother of the correct punctuation is less
cumbersome.

Usually, 8th graders have already learned about the proper use of
punctuation, just as they have learned about semi-colons, sentence

fragments, indentation, paragraph construction and a host of other useful grammatical and stylistic features of good writing. Inevitably, however, the rules don't stick until they are yet again broached in high school. High school English teachers can never believe how unprepared the incoming 8th graders are—in a school lucky enough to have its own high school—and they mumble and grumble and wonder what in the world these children ever learned from their class teacher. The process is a bit like gardening. The first time the seeds flower, they often produce unspectacular results. Eventually there will be a glorious bush of brilliant blossoms—if we've tended the plant. Not rarely does the nascent writer flourish in 11th grade. And even then, s/he may still be confused about quotation marks.

To provide the students with some experience of how necessary quotation marks are, I like to give them something like this:

> lets exclaimed Scotty he was pointing at the black dog please mom lets get the black one he repeated she frowned dont you think one is enough she asked oh no mom you cant have too many dogs well she said who will keep their water clean will you

or:

> watch out dad shouted Julia scrambling over the slick grey rocks these rocks are really slippery I'll live dad replied twisting around to smile at his daughter Look here Julie I found a turtle whoa that is a big one the girl said can we keep him dad please no dear answered her father ruffling Julia's blond curls this is a wild thing he explained and you always leave wild things where they belong

"Please stop doing that annoying quote marks thing."

There will be one or two students who relish sorting out a mess like this, but if too many of your students are likely to sink into the quagmire hopelessly, then provide them with some clues. Perhaps in their version the sentences will have a capital letter to start and a period to end.

Having worked on the dialogues, possibly even performed them, having seen how indispensable quotation marks are, we now have to practice using them, with all their punctuation requirements, and for that, we'll have to come up with more exercises.

It's important to work on these exercises slowly enough, so that we can really explain the details without rushing. And let's not underestimate the extent to which we need to repeat the exercises, correct them, find different ways to get at the problem. Humor can be a real help here, because the confusion resulting from misused quotation marks or their total lack can be hilarious.

Once we feel we've got a handle on the quotation marks, we can have a few exercises in which we combine the pesky confusing words with the equally pesky quotation marks. These sentences would be dictated:

1. Where were you?
2. Their excitement about the game was great.
3. "It's too bad you missed it!" exclaimed my teacher.
4. "Two of them," said Joe, "were there too."
5. Each playing field has its beauty.
6. They're on their way to the championship.
7. Two of them went too far.
8. "I," said the captain of the team, "can come too."
9. "It's late," said the coach. "Time to quit."
10. "Where were you during the game?" I asked.

1. I know it's here.
2. Where were their books?
3. They're late again.
4. It's a good idea.
5. What is its price?
6. "That's too bad," she said to the two girls.
7. "I thought," said Bob, "the twins were there too."
8. You're wasting too much time.
9. He lost its cover.
10. That dog loves its bone.

The Fallacy of the Adjective

If I ever have to read about another red apple, blue sky or nice anything, I will use my red ink, be blue in the face, and not be nice at all.

Clichés

Sometimes it's really right to remind your reader that the sky is blue. Out here in northern California, it rarely needs mentioning because sea breezes and clear skies are the norm. Possibly, if we're describing the snow on Fifth Avenue right after a blizzard, we might want to let the reader know that white snow glistens as Billy tries out his new cross-country skis. But please, let the snow be white only when it needs to be mentioned, and, please, let's not have it "blanket" anything.

How can we avoid clichés? First, of course, we have to recognize them. If the phrase jumps into our mind before we've even tried to formulate it, then we can be pretty sure it's been used a million times and, having been used so often, has lost its charm. That doesn't mean it can never be used. There are legitimate reasons to mention that the grass is green, the child is small, or the house is big. But most of the time, the inexperienced writer is not really engaged when s/he resorts to time-worn expressions.

Here is a comprehensive, amusing attempt at a definition:

A cliché is a traditional form of human expression (in words, thoughts, emotions, gestures, acts) which—due to repetitive use in social life—has lost its original, often ingenious heuristic power. Although it thus fails positively to contribute meaning to social interactions and communication, it does function socially, since it manages to stimulate behavior (cognition, emotion, volition, action), while it avoids reflection on meanings.[22]

We needn't foist such a definition on our middle school students; they get the idea very quickly after just a few examples. Let's make a list of adjectival clichés:

White snow, blue sky, red apple, green grass, big house, small child, tall mountain, deep valley...

Yes, they are redundant, common, obvious. As writers, we need a more discriminating use of modifiers. What's a modifier? It's a descriptive word or phrase that tells you more about the thing it modifies.

Child, mountain, house, grass... these are generic words. We spent a lot of time at the start of our course on learning to come up with less generic, more specific words, and we focused on the nouns and the verbs. Adjectives, too, need scrutiny. Sprinkling adjectives throughout our writing as if they were fertilizer meant to enrich our descriptions, simply leads to droopy seedlings, best weeded out.

14 Rule Number Fourteen:
Be judicious in your use of modifiers. First find the most specific noun; then, if needed, add an original adjective. Find the most specific verb; then, if needed, add a spicy adverb.

Adverbs are also modifiers, but because we are more likely to reach for a precise verb, we are less likely to overuse adverbs.

How did the adjective myth gain such currency? Why do beginning writers think that florid writing elevates their prose? Possibly because it's easier to use a tired, overused, dull, tasteless, pablum-like adjective than a feisty, frolicking, original, illuminating one.

Adhering to an adjective diet can be a revelation. The following piece of writing was the solution to this assignment: Write a three-part description—setting, character(s) and action, conclusion—using no more than two modifiers. This writer was a 10th grader.

Impression

The silhouettes of the pines lean into the gale. The branches brush each other and wail like violins. Cones tumble into the snow; snowflakes cascade in flurries through the air. The reeds by the pond sway and bob like a troupe of dancers.

The colors of the children's scarves brighten the ice. As they skate they clutch each other to stop themselves from stumbling. They shriek in merriment and fun. Tumbling and falling one over the other, they crash in heaps onto the ice. They race and chase each other, and their skates flash as they vanish into the distance.

The ice remains, the surface scratched and marred by frantic blades, and above, the pines still wail.[23]

Writers and storytellers since the time of Homer have avoided the tired adjective by using literary devices, in which one thing is compared to another. There are mainly three types: simile, metaphor and personification.

Simile and Metaphor

Although 8th graders can grasp the architecture of a simile, metaphor is something they can usually only ape. By the time 10th, 11th or 12th graders read *Moby Dick*, they can embrace the concept of white whale as more than white whale; they can comprehend the symbolic, analogous nature of the great struggle between Ahab and the whale. 8th graders, on the other hand, when asked what the meaning of the old man's struggle in *The Old Man and the Sea* might represent, are generally clueless, though the more glib amongst them can fluently tell you it's a story about life's struggles. When asked whether the old man won or lost his struggle, some 8th graders sound wise. But hardly a one can support the judgment with details from the book. They're just swimming about in the sound of it all. Here, for example, are a few responses to the question, Did you like the story overall? If so, why? If not, why not? This was the only part of the "block review" or final test in which opinion was solicited.

> Compared to other school books, I liked this one because it has a basic but interesting story and is easy to read. *[by an excellent student]*
> I didn't think it was that interesting how it was written. And it was a little sad. *[by a very good writer]*
> I enjoyed the different writing style and the creativity of the story. I think the story had many lessons and virtues to teach. *[by a very proficient writer]*

Not even the most capable students remarked on the story, let alone its Pulitzer Prize-winning heroics.

Similes, on the other hand, are more easily recognized, more easily understood. Our language is littered with them. So, as with the adjectives, we need to become aware of similes which are clichés, as worn out as your favorite shirt.

Here again a list is useful. It should go into the binder, and after you've provided a few examples for the students, let them continue the list. It will be a good exercise to see whether it's obvious when a simile is a cliché.

> He was as strong as an ox.
> She was as light as a feather.
> The twins were as alike as two peas in a pod.
> The night sky was as black as pitch.
> My garden is as dry as dust.
> Her eyes were like stars.

We've heard these before, they are almost like proverbs, familiar sayings that are just part of our language. Good writers avoid clichés in any form, especially when they are similes that are as familiar as a nursery rhyme. Of course, if a writer is putting such tired words in the mouth of a character, that's a different story.

Poets excel at inventing new similes. That's a big part of what makes them poets. We'll look at some examples of similes by famous poets after we've worked on writing them ourselves.

Children enjoy the challenge of completing similes. If you provide an intriguing springboard, amazing flights of comparison can result. I provided the following example:

His story was like a fruit salad, all mixed up.
Her story was like Wonder bread, mushy and insipid.

And here are some of the 8th graders' results:

His story was like a straw hat, nicely woven together.
His story was like a rain forest, dense and colorful.
His story was like a Wyland painting, beautiful and inspiring.
His story was like a person in a crowded room, way hard to
   follow.
Her story was like a child's scream, painful to the ear.
His story was like my attempts at writing this simile: full of
   promise, but yielding unfortunate results.
His story was like a stream with twists and turns.

Or, another given example:

His explanation was as likely as a rose garden in the desert.

This yielded:

His explanation was as dull as a blunt pencil.
His explanation was as touching as a hero's last words.
His explanation was as predictable as the cycles of the moon.
His explanation was as contorted as a pretzel.
Her explanation was as confusing as learning Chinese is
   for a Turk.

Unexpectedly profound results came from the conclusion to
"Life is like…"

Life is like a confectionery shop, sour and sweet, but it's all candy.
Life is like gambling; you never know what you'll get.
Life is like fruit; it can be sweet but it can go sour.

Life is like a river; you can always hit a waterfall.
Life is like a wheel; it rolls and rolls until it hits a bump.
Life is like outer space, filled with mystery and wonder.

We also tackled, "His face looked like…"

His face looked like a battered canvas kite, torn and bleeding.
His face looked like a complicated book with tiny print, quite
hard to read.

During this segment of our studies, we also paid attention to the many similes Hemingway used in the story we were reading. We took a moment to consider their effectiveness. For example:

The old man: None of these scars was fresh. They were as old as
erosions in a fishless desert.
The marlin: His sword was as long as a baseball bat and tapered
like a rapier and he rose his full length from the water and
then re-entered it, smoothly, like a diver…

A couple of times, I handed out a sheet of incomplete similes and had the students complete them. We then collected and considered the results:

The cat slid through the undergrowth as silently as…
When her pet mouse died, she was as sad as …
Eating ice cream on a hot summer day is like …
Having to do homework on the weekend is like …
The wind howled in the trees like …

We tried to gauge the comparison on a "cliché meter," a line on the board with one end labeled "cliché" and the other end labeled "original." Once again the conclusions were obvious and the students reached consensus easily.

The task of coming up with a simile instead of an adjective to describe the following features of a character in a story inspired a particularly savvy student to the following:

Hair: The zoologist's hair was like that of a mandrill, long and shaggy.

Hands: The journalist's hands were as smooth as the computer screen he stared at.

Shoes: The ornithologist's shoes were as well-traveled as the wind.

Voice: When the gardener spoke, her voice was like rain falling from the leaves of a tree.

Clearly, this young man, an excellent student, enjoyed the task.

Before leaving the realm of simile, let's look at examples of similes by well-established poets. Now that we've struggled to come up with apt, original similes, we'll be able to appreciate the precision and inventiveness of these pictures. We might even ask the students to complete these famous poets' similes before revealing how the poets did it.

"The dragonfly was like…"
"The breaths of the horses were like…"

Deep in the sun-searched growths the dragon-fly
Hangs like a blue thread against the sky…
　　　　　　　– Dante Gabriel Rossetti

And then Llewellyn leapt and fled
Like one with hornets in his hair…
　　　　　　　– Edwin Arlington Robinson

A ragman passed with his horses, their breaths
Blooming like white peonies…
– Donald Hall

The clouds travel like white handkerchiefs of goodbye.
– Pablo Neruda (translated by W.S. Merwin)

Personification

Why do I forbid personification? Because inexperienced writers, especially young ones, mistakenly think that when a flower smiles or the wind breathes, it is automatically poetic and profound. Most of the time though, such human attributes superimposed on inanimate objects are inexact and trite. Of course there is a wealth of possibility in using this figure of speech, but because it so quickly veers into sentimentality and superficiality, it requires some care. Better to wait until the student writers are capable of discernment. 10th grade would be a good time to introduce it, possibly 11th. It would fit nicely with a lyric poetry block.

15 *Rule Number Fifteen:*
Do not use personification.

A quick Google search provides a bounty of unappealing examples:

The stars danced playfully in the moonlit sky.
The run-down house appeared depressed.
The first rays of morning tiptoed through the meadow.[24]

There are 47 more where these came from. On the other hand, Google also gives us a plethora of worthy examples by established writers:

> I hied me away to the woods—away back into the sun-washed alleys carpeted with fallen gold and glades where the moss is green and vivid yet. The woods are getting ready to sleep—they are not yet asleep but they are disrobing and are having all sorts of little bed-time conferences and whisperings and good-nights.
> – From L.M. Montgomery's "The Green Gables Letters"

> When well-appareled April on the heel
> Of limping winter treads.
> – From Shakespeare's *Romeo and Juliet*, Act I, Scene 2

> Loveliest of trees, the cherry now
> Is hung with bloom along the bough,
> And stands about the woodland ride
> Wearing white for Eastertide.
> – From "Loveliest of Trees the Cherry Now"
>   by A.E. Housman

> Have you got a brook in your little heart,
> Where bashful flowers blow,
> And blushing birds go down to drink,
> And shadows tremble so?
> – Emily Dickinson

It's not that personification is unappealing, just that it so easily gets maudlin. Determining whether a figure of speech is successful or merely a diversionary ploy takes some judgment. By high school or amongst adults, arguments on the merits of each case might be helpful. For upper elementary school students, however, I'd rather just avoid this nest of snakes.

What's more, by prohibiting personification, we sensitize our students to this device. We prevent glib and generally unsuccessful characterization. We save it for later when our students can appreciate why "bashful flowers" and "blushing birds" took some thought by the poet. We wait until our students can marvel at the precision and inventiveness of "When well-appareled April on the heel of limping winter treads."

Again, as with any of the literary devices we've considered, if we come across personification in our reading, we might stop to consider the effect. Is it helpful? Why did the writer use this device just here?

Write On!

While taking the time at the beginning of each main lesson (20–30 minutes or so if it's a two-hour class) to consider and review the details we need to master by working through a variety of what I call "In-Class Exercises," we also use class time to write short stories. By allotting a good measure of class time to writing, we avoid the potential of any type of at-home assistance, whether personal or technological. Students who lack confidence benefit the most from having to write on their own, with no help apart from a dictionary.

Having progressed from stories in one sentence through stories in three sentences and then to paragraphs, we then apply what we've learned to the real thing: the short story. We've been working on stories all along of course, always with a particular purpose, whether to practice the turning point, or characterization, or word choice and so forth.

Although we are now working on the story as a whole, without a particular technical focal point, I still provide a general direction. For example: The setting is a park. The writer needs to establish the time of day and the weather. The character should develop out of the setting.

Here is a story (errors and all) by an extremely reluctant student, the type of student who has little self-esteem when it comes to academics, and consequently has perfected the sassy, "I'm-not-interested-in-whatever-you-have-to-offer" attitude. In spite of herself, she was drawn into our work and wrote from the heart:

It is dark now the swings are rocking themselvies in the crisp wind. The tire swing is being spon by the wind in a rythmic circle. Big rain clouds began to take over the sky and it starts to rain. This rain makes the paint on the monkey bars start to slide down on to the wood chips. With tears streaming down his face and a teddy bear in hand a little boy sprinted to the park. Spining on the tire swing thinking of what has just happened and gripes his teddy bear and wipes the tears of his face and ran into the darkness.

What a picture of this girl's inner life. She hasn't told us why the little boy is crying, but the details are inhabited and the mood is strong. It's convincing. She has revealed something of herself. She did not want her work read to her classmates. Of course I honored her request.

Another "Park" story, this one by a boy who often arrived at school late, who often didn't do his homework on time, whose handwriting was difficult to read. In class he minded his manners and often raised his hand to answer questions correctly. A popular chap, during the breaks he was always on the cusp of making trouble, given the chance. He discovered that he enjoyed writing. Technically, his writing was deficient, but he lived into his work, and all aspects of his writing improved rapidly over our four weeks together. Most impressively, by the middle of week three, he got to school on time, with his homework done. Again, errors have not been corrected.

A layer of soft, white snow rests a top the ground where Rabbits and weazles can be found. The trees around this Park have a frosty coat about their leaves. While the light still shines brightly through Branches causing the frost glisten in the light. The lake next to the park is frozen over, with tracks of ice skates piercing the ice. A gentile Breeze flows through the park, lightly swaying the smaller trees. Little Birds can be seen flying through the cold, crisp air while squirrels leap from tree to tree. Rocks are present, but not always seen. Only the larger rocks peer through the snow. In the distance, snow-capped mountains stand above the park and even glaciers are visible from certain areas. Over head the sky is Blue with little clouds scattered across the sky and a Bright yellow sun blazing in the blue. The park eventually woke up and other people started to come and have fun in the park. One small child seemed to have the most fun he would go and to get as close as he could to one of the animals. This young child seemed to have a talent because he could get extremely close to the birds. The birds seemed to not be scared of the child. The boy continued to do this for a while until he got tired. When he got tired, him and his mother continued on to their next thing in that day.

Tenderness is being expressed here. And the longing to return to paradise where we can be close to the birds. The cadence of the sentences moves along engagingly. When I read this aloud to his classmates, the boy's eyes grew wide. He himself didn't realize how well it worked. As I read it, I ignored the syntactical mistakes, the weak spots. Nor did I point out the subtleties of mood and cadence, which would have most likely embarrassed him. Instead, I mentioned the technical successes: the transitions, the careful choice of words. On his paper, I commented that it's high time to stop using capital letters so randomly. We can see, also, how his inner eye flagged toward the end. Above "their next thing" I commented: *generic!* Next to "...the light shines brightly through Branches causing the frost to glisten in the light," I wrote: *Nice!*

For a different take, let's look at an example by an "imagination poor" youngster. The writer is an ambitious girl who wants to please:

A Park

[You can't get more generic than that for a title, indicating that from the get-go, our writer's imagination is not fired up.]

> Trees line the curved path around the grass. Nearby, a fountain bubbles. Water in the fountain glistens in the bright morning sun. Birds quietly chirp in the trees, while squirrels scamper across the park. The sharp sunlight cuts *[ah!]* through the trees, rays of light landing on the path. The grass is wet, and sparkles in the sunlight.
>
> A young schoolboy dashes *[hooray]* into the park. He wanders for a bit, then stops at the fountain. He stares up at the figures, then makes a decision. He gets a coin, tosses it in the fountain, and watches it slowly sink to the bottom. Skipping back to the grass, he lies down and watches the clouds.

Well, you may think, what's wrong with that? Technically, it's flawless. Nothing is wrong with it. But it is really just one cliché after another. The writer is successfully applying our don't-start-with-*The* rule, and that's good. She is avoiding *walk*, and that's good. She is not doing so well with the transitions: fountains, birds, sunlight, grass. She slides from one to the next and uses words which sound right. However, the overall result is template-like. Generic. Here is the relatively rare occasion for a ✓+/✓- ; a plus for technicalities, a minus for content. (See page 168 for an explanation of these marks.)

In fact, though, this assignment received only one mark, and hers was a check without a comment. I did not want to discourage her. Praise, however, was equally uncalled for.

Our next writer is a boy whose "Paragraph About Myself" started like this:

> I like to play Baseball and Football. Also, I like to shoot guns and bows. Working out and doing martial arts are very fun […] I hope I get into West Point and study law or medicine. If I get accepted I would serve in the military as a doctor or lawyer to pay off my tuition.

"I like to shoot bows," was a bit of an understatement. He was a state champion. English was not his first language, but that did not prevent him from shooting off his mouth until I produced my "Class Participation" chart. Short on imagination, he was long on pragmatism. His park:

Park in Winter

> The deserted park is covered in the newly [sic] fallen snow. The only light comes from an old street lamp. One could hear birds, crickets, and the distant howl of wolves. A nearby lake is frozen from the chill, and when the sun rises one could spot happy children ice scating [sic] on it.

He has dutifully done what he was asked to do. But he has not noticed that he has placed crickets into a chilly night, or that while wolves are howling, birds are chirping. And hard to spot in the dawn light, those children sure are out early! Eventually, this writer produced a long, intricate thriller-type story, which started off: "Three black Escalades pulled into the secret army base." His title: "The Heroic Actions of Four Men That Led to the Capture of a Ruthless Dictator." The name of the "team commander" was almost the same as his own.

Finally, here is the "park" by a very imaginative, sophisticated and self-confident writer who, knowing that adults had little to offer the likes of her, only grudgingly got on board our literary ship.

In-Class Exercise

Green & yellow cypress trees, spaced evenly around the worn, cement path seem to strech their limbs welcoming the first, crisp lights of spring. Park benches, scratched from years of family photos and tourist's picknick lunches, scatter the park, providing a perfect view of the NYC skyline. The familiar sprint-time chill stings the green, trimmed grass, freezing the droplets of morning due. At the base of a sign reading Straberry Feilds, a worn, leather guitar case sits opne, luering spare change from the pockets of us morning wonderers.

I come here often, to strawberry fields, twice a day actually. *[several sentences scratched out]*

Strawberry feilds is a space for me to un-wind. It lets me escape from the tourist ivaded SoHo. As the familiar Beetle's tunes fill my mind and calm my nerus, I can actually think. I Kneel down in front of Chris, the owner of the old, black guitar case. His eyes are closed, as he moves to the music flowing from his guitar. As the sound of music is replaced by light applause, Chrises eyes open and he notices me. "Hey there!" he says "You're up early today." I take a deep sigh. "Yeah well I couldnt fall back to sleep and I can never focus in that claustraphobic apartment, so I just came out here. Helps me think." Chris nods understandingly. It's a kind of starving-artist to starving-artist connection we have. I have known Chris for three and a half years now, thanks to my frequent trips to Central Park, and his John-Lennon-honoring, street performing. Chris is by far my best-friend in New York. "Wanna join me for lunch today? I have been dying to talk to you, there is something I really need to tell you. We don't have to go anywhere special, maybe Rustic Bakery?" I eye Chris cautiously, "Ohkaaay…" I say. That is when I begin to feel an uneasy feeling building up in my chest. What if he can't come to strawberry fields anymore? What if he's moving. After a moment of Chris looking at me apprehensively and me feeling queasy as if I had just gotten off a roller coaster, I tuck a loose strand of my blonde hair behind my ear and smile. "That sounds great! I will see you then, yes?" I give Chris a hug and then wander back the way I had come, the feeling of fear still nagging at my insides. Little did I know that "sit-on-the-corner-w-my-guitar Chris" was about to bring the opportunity of a lifetime.

So much adolescent yearning! So touchingly young in spite of the worldly knowingness.

Every now and then there will be a quiet, mature, highly capable student who hands in a story that astonishes you with its depths. Such students may already have an excellent grip on the grammar, punctuation, syntax or vocabulary touched on in this writing block. They may even have had a natural sense for transitions and turning points before you introduced these concepts to the class. Such a student may rise into, and bear witness imaginatively to, a realm she already surveys, although she is only an 8th grader and surrounded by the motley crew of less mature classmates.

The assignment was given in the last week of the block which happened to be the week before the Christmas holiday. The task was to write a story which starts in the darkness and ends in the light. And of course all the elements we'd worked on throughout the block were to be employed.

A Mother's Pain

Nani never got to see her face.

She remembers the pain, lasting hours and hours. She had clutched the nurse's hands so tightly that they were red and bruised by the time it was over. Nani hadn't even planned on keeping her, she had just wanted to be able to hold her in her arms once. She had wanted to be able to look in her baby's eyes and feel her chubby, little fingers curl around her larger ones.

Nani had waited to hear the first cries of her child, she had been anticipating them. They would be loud and healthy, the kid would have a good set of lungs. But the cries never came and that is when Nani knew something was wrong.

She can still remember that moment in all of its excruciating detail. Her hair had been sticking to her forehead and neck, the long dark strands soaked with sweat. Her blue hospital gown was creased and tears still pricked her eyes whenever she saw that particular shade. The lights were so bright that they hurt. She had wanted to tell them to turn them down, but she had been in too much pain. And then the horrible hush. The nurse had tightened her hold on Nani's hand and the midwife's face had been grim and weary.

There was no sound of crying. No baby being hoisted up into the air to be cocooned in a warm blanked and place into the waiting arms of their mother. Instead there were the midwife and nurses saying, sorry, "Your baby's dead." It was then that she had started to scream and cry. She let out all the paint, and the fears and the tears that had been collecting for so long. She screamed for her mother, who had tried so hard, for the father she had never known. She screamed at the dirty looks she had received and the disappointed gazes of her teachers and peers, at God in Heaven and the Devil in Hell and everything in between, but mostly Nani had screamed for her baby, for her beautiful little girl that she had never even seen.

But that was years ago. There was better technology now, better medicine. But still, the white sterility of the hospital makes her feel sick, the blue gowns had not changed and the lights were still too bright. Nani feel in her gut, the deep ache of worry, but still, she goes through the pain and breathes in and out, and this time there is someone there to hold her had who is not a nurse. There is a moment when she is terrified that she can't breathe. Her mouth opens and no sound comes out, and then she hears it: the high wail of a newborn child. There are tears covering her hot cheeks and that sound, the sound of her healthy child. That is the most beautiful sound she has ever heard.

Is it melodramatic? Perhaps, but there is real talent here, and this writer took the opportunity to reveal the adolescent drama of the soul which I never glimpsed in class. The writer, now in high school, responded to my request for a comment about this story with the following:

I don't remember much about writing "A Mother's Pain," which was my "coming from the darkness into the light" story, but I do remember that I Googled *stillbirth* and I saw all these pictures of little, barely developed babies that were dead and I think I just started crying. I channeled a lot of that into writing the story.

Just as well that I didn't know about the Googling part, although to her credit, the writer had the idea of the subject and then Googled it, not the other way around.

An 8th grade boy fighting off depression submitted the following as his Darkness into Light story (his spelling left intact).

The morning sun was shinning through the wisps of fluffy cloud, making every bead of dew sparkle. Everything was fresh, green and lush. The air felt cold and crisp. A gentle breeze blew. Birds sang in the trees. Merry groups of people strolled up and down the park paths, smiling.

Alex's surroundings could not penetrate his emotions. He did not feel the sun. He did not appreciate the scenery. He was absorbed in the black chasm inside his chest where winds of sadness howled and clouds blocked the sky. Alex did not care that he should be rejoicing on this day of cellebration. He sat on a bench in the shade of a tree, in his own sphere as people brushed past him.

He wore stained gray sweatpants and sneakers. A black hoodie covered his face so that the only thing one could see was his stubbly, unshaven chin. He slouched with his hands in his pocket.

All of the sudden he had an urge to look up. When he did, he saw his friend James running towards him through the grass. He looked fresh and wore a massive grin. He appeared to Alex like an angel. "Hey! I've been looking all over for you." At this moment, something suddenly lifted in Alex's heart. His friend did not ask what he was doing or judge him at all. He simply smiled. "Lets head over to your apartment so you can shower and then we'll find something for you to wear. then, maybe you can come over to my place and help me set up. I am hosting a party this evening and I have a feeling the party is going to be awesome." "Sure," replied Alex. He stood up and removed his hood. All of a sudden he felt overwhelmingly happy. He appreciated James so much. Matter a fact he appreciated everything. As the two walked down the path, Alex felt the sunshine and he let it into his soul.

This boy was a wonderful cellist. Mostly silent in class, he often gazed at me with earnest intensity. His story doesn't have the depth or maturity of the childbirth story which precedes it, and sentence by sentence much could be improved, but his story conveys— economically and pictorially; indeed, artistically—the volatility and vulnerability of the teenage soul, his own.

Here is yet another piece on the theme of Darkness into the Light. This writer was not keen on writing. Yet, by making use of what we'd worked on, he produced a story with all the elements we had studied. Setting, character, turning point, resolution. He avoided starting every sentence with *The*. And he has learned how to convey the story through pictures.

In the high desert, the sun was just rising. Purple, orange, pink and blue streaked accross the sky. Bright red sand framed the picture, and shrubs dotted the landscape.

Then a shadow crept into view. The man that came with it was skinny and tall and wore long indigo robes. Under the beaking sun, the man made slow progress.

Then out of the distance a cloud of fire appeared, a sandstorm. The man pulled a scarf over his head and put on his gogles. When the sandstorm hit him it was like a million tiny bullets. He was dazed and confused, spun around and totally disoriented.

When the storm passed, the man was faceing a random direction and totally lost. Despite his odds of survival, he trudged through the sand.

Then in the night, the man saw a pultruding silhoets and the light of a fire. At first he thought is was a mirage, but as he approached the sound of nomad camp filled the air. They took him in and fed him. Hope was not lost.

Indeed, hope was not lost. Often, during the years that I've taught youngsters to write, I've been touched by the optimism, positivity and hopefulness that their stories convey. Bullets bounce harmlessly, fish are released, bones mend, friends forgive, fame calls, adventure ends well.

Such tendencies are encouraged when the task at hand is the writing itself rather than the story. True, for several of the stories above, the task was to bring the character in the story out of the darkness and into the light. But even when that is not articulated as a goal, the stories are often idealistic stories of success. For example:

Red Carpet Girl

It's a cold morning in paris. *[Sigh. Not the best first sentence. Never mind. Lower case "paris." No excuse for that.]* The smell of crepês *[There's an accent somewhere in this word.]* wafted through the crisp air and birds flitted about, scraping the ground with their tiny *[well observed]* feet, looking for morsel of food people dropped. As people *[circle the repeated word]* started bustling *[nice!]* through the streets, the birds scattered, soaring in random *[hmm. Do little birds soar?]* directions. As *[circle – Avoid starting sentences with same word.]* one landed on the windowsill of a building across the street *[punctuation]* *[But she's remembering transitions.]* a twenty-one year old girl rushed *[good, another alternative to "walked"]* out of an apartment and into the street. Her hair was raven black, and her skin as pale as white marble *[okay, not the most original figure of speech, but a figure of speech nonetheless. I just wish she could have said something like "Her raven black hair surrounded her pale face," anything but "Her hair was...."]* She was in a hurry to eat before she had to rush off to class. As the girl stopped at a crepe *[Gone is the gratuitous accent.]* stand, the crepe maker might be able to see her chocolaty brown eyes and the beauty mark on her collar bone, making her seem more fragile *[mixed-up tenses, but she is trying to give details about the character—something we'd practiced a lot]*. After eating the crepe, she scurried down two blocks, dodging people left and right. She walked *[Okay, this seems a good place to use the generic "walk."]* into the building. As she hurried through a hallway, she passed a sign that read "Welcome to Parsons Paris." *[need to circle the closing quotation mark because the period is directly under it— hedging the bets of where to place it]* The girl was wearing *[ugh, very hard to break that "was ___ing" formula]* a rosy pink skirt that stopped two inches above her knees, a white longsleeve cashmere v-neck, and a pair of tan boots with white knee socks. *[The clothing description seems out of place, but never mind. Clearly, she is trying to include the ingredients we discussed in class.]* She passed a few people and walked into her Product Design class, *[comma?]* just before the bell rang. The girl's name was Kat. Kat was a

senior in Parsons and Majoring *[sic]* in Fashion Design. She would graduate in two days. Kat was quite busy but *[?]* she had a true talent for design, creating dresses nobody had dreamed of. Kat was born in New York and lived there until Sophomore year of high school, when she travled *[sic]* to Paris to learn French *[both proper nouns capitalized as afterthoughts with heavy strokes of the pen]*. She had instantly fallen in love with the city, the language, and culture.

Two days later Katherine-Elise graduated. She was happy and sad, her years at Parsons flew by *[tense mix-up]*. As she left school, after picking up her sewing machine *[nice!]* and walked back to her apartment. *[Whoa, this is an incomplete sentence.]* When she walked in a pile of envalopes *[sic]* skidded across the floor. She picked them up after setting her sewing machine aside. *[Good, the imagination is at work for her to include this detail.]* One enalope *[sic]* especialy *[sic]* made her curious. She opened it. It was from a well known woman who needed a dress for the red carpet within two months. Kat was so excited she almost screamed. That night she got the womens *[sic and sic]* measurements and got to work the next day. Three weeks later Kat shipped the dress to her. The woman was overjoyed by the dress and recommended "Kat-Elise" to friends of hers. Kat was on her way after all her hard work for the past five years.

For this girl, this was a breakthrough. She put something of herself into that story, and the deficiencies in spelling and grammar and punctuation and sequence are less important than that she invested something of herself for the assignment.

I asked this particular class to write a "Paragraph About Myself." This was not to be the usual type of assignment, because I was not going to evaluate it, nor was I going to return it to them. I suggested they tell me about activities they currently enjoy, as well as what they think they might end up doing in the future.

The girl who wrote about "Kat-Elise" handed in the following. (To protect her identity, I've replaced revealing facts with blanks.)

> I currently go to _____ Waldorf School. I am in 8th grade. After school I like to play Lacrosse and go to dance class. I play lacrosse on the U-15 team for _____ [town where she lives]. My dance studio is called Love2Dance and I do Hip Hop there.
>
> I want to go to high school at _____ for dance. The audition is in less than two weeks and I'm very nervous.
>
> _____ School also has an amazing lacrosse team which I would try out for, even though not very many freshmen get on the team.
>
> I'm not sure where I want to go to college, but I do want to go to college. Preferably I would be able to see my family. I want to be either a dancer, or something in the fashion business. My back up plan is a doctor or nurse. Or a veterinarian for horses.

This girl rarely looked up during class. Her gaze was always directed down at her desk. The minute class ended, she was surrounded by other girls. She had a boyfriend, a fellow student. They had been told by their regular class teacher that they weren't to be boyfriend and girlfriend during school hours, and from what I observed, they kept to that. She tried more than once to test the limits of what the school allowed by way of makeup; the dress code inspired her too. Her "Paragraph About Myself" is so poignantly immature. Her story about Kat-Elise and her thoughts about herself are made of the same stuff: a vague, youthful desire for success. This girl lacked a strong sense of her own identity, but as the weeks of our course progressed, she became more and more engaged, until she actually fulfilled a writing assignment with a piece that meant something to her.

A story I cherished came from a short, choleric boy who lacked writing finesse, wrote sloppily in all respects, and tended to be loud in class; it contains the same yearning for recognition as the previous story, though the theme is very different. (I have only the corrected copy, so many of the misspellings and other technical shortcomings are no longer available, although there are still some that remained in the version printed here.) The story was submitted with a ballpoint cover drawing which I had not asked for, and the pages were bound with stitched thread. My heart leapt up when he handed it in.

Antonio Rossi

On a hill, stood the most beautiful house in Palermo, Italy. It belonged to the motor GP racer, Antonio Rossi. It had a beautiful front yard, a marble fountain in the middle, a pool to the left, with a hot tub on the upper left corner of the pool. There was a grand hall for an entrance and doors to the left and right heading to many rooms and areas of the house. In the backyard of the house, there was a grill and outdoor seating where Antonio liked to have parties and cook for his friends. The interior of the house was at least the same level beauty of the rest of the property if not more.

Everything was hand-picked and modified to fit the shape and theme of the house.

Every morning Antonio would put on his favorite green and black Patagonia bathing suite and take a dip his beautiful cold pool with his family. Antonio's family knew that he loved architecture and interior design but they knew that he did love racing, especially the difficult tracks.

Antonio's work as an architect and designer really was amazing. It was so good that some off his close friends who knew about his passion asked him to make custom pieces for their houses. Mr. Rossi's house also had a personal gym which was used every day to stay fit for his races. He also loved to play tennis, so often he would set up a net in his back yard and play tennis with his family, friends as well as colligues.

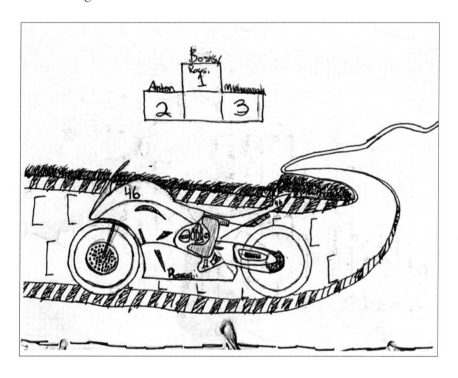

The master Motor GP racer had a Grand Prix which was a difficult track, with hairpin turns on an incline and all sorts of other obstacles. Antonio had beaten all the other racers and come in at 1st place which was a big deal since it was the last race of the season, but when the camera came to Mr. Rossi and asked him why he was not thrilled with his victory, he said: "Because racing is not my passion."

Antonio started a career in design and architecture but was still a racer as a 2nd job. Antonio started small as a normal person would. He made custom pieces for people who asked. He advritised himself through fliers and a website.

In no time Antonio had started a byissness which was thriving very often with wealthy customers.

The End

Here was a piece of writing, which, whatever its merits, had elevated this boy's imagination out of the roar of the motorcycle track and into the luxurious, successful and precisely seen country home of Antonio Rossi. Like our writer, there was much more to Mr. Rossi than just speed and noise. He had high standards, he had lofty ambitions. He "started small" and he prevailed.

Sometimes the least gifted students provide us with the best gifts. Then again, there are the well-veneered, able students, who bequeath on us a glimpse of a hidden soul.

In their "Paragraph About Myself," many of the 8th graders in that robust class of 25 students mentioned sports, or other hobbies such as ballet, as their career goals. Some professed confusion about their future. "My goal is to learn and have fun" is not atypical of their mood. However, "My goal is to attend a UC school" came from a young man who listed as his interests and hobbies: tennis, basketball, flight simulation "where I use a Bluetooth joystick with a button I have programmed to different tasks," computer programming, bowling and table tennis. "In high school, I plan on continuing to pursue my interest in computer programming. I also expect to take four years of math at a fairly accelerated level instead of the required three years." He concludes his error-free composition with, "However, my interests may change."

Whether that last sentence indicates an escape hatch or just common sense, this boy's writing was always technically flawless and thematically mature. Here is one of his final stories. Like Jamie of 40 years earlier, the writer expresses compassion for the natural world so keenly observed. We know that Jamie, now James, became a successful, well-respected steward of the oceans and its creatures as a professional oceanographer. The writer of "A Hunter's Wish" has a wide-open future, but having once given voice to the tenderness within, he is more likely to engage with it again.

A Hunter's Wish

Dark gray storm clouds loomed over the rain-soaked forest. Leaves on the tall pines rustled with the chilly breeze. The trees formed a circular clearing, revealing the forest floor littered with fallen twigs and bark. A tall young man pushed through the dense bushes and marched into the open space. His shiny gray eyes blazed from under his crooked leather cap covering his light brown hair, as his dark eyebrows furrowed in a frown. He wore an army green vest over a long-sleeved white shirt which hung much too big for his thin torso. Brown cloth pants extended only to the knee where they met his tall white socks and his hard-heeled hunting boots. In his right hand, he carried a small rifle.

His gaze darted in many directions as he twisted the ends of his long mustache. Soon his eyes rested on faded deer tracks leading away from the clearing. With a glint of suspicion and satisfaction in his expression, he began to follow the tracks and strode away from the patch of open ground. The tracks led him back into the forest winding between trees and around patches of brush. As he pushed past the greenery, heavy droplets of rainwater that clung to the leaves and branches were shaken off. They fell silently and landed on the man's shirt, soaking the white sleeves that ran down from his leather vest. However, he ignored their cold and discomfort as he continued to trudge ahead, leaving footsteps closely tracking those of the deer.

His feet grew weary in their boots as he marched for hours squinting carefully ahead of the deer tracks for a sign of the animal. As he looked up at the sky, he could see that the afternoon was growing late. The sun was beginning to fall behind the dense layer of clouds. He knew that he must get home before sundown. However, his only wish was to catch a deer in the woods. He had caught rabbits and other small game since he was a teenager, but he knew that now he had a good chance of catching a deer.

The hoof prints in the forest soon became more pronounced, and the man knew that they were fresh, less worn away by rain and wind. Ahead of him, he spotted another open clearing among the trees and, eying it carefully, thought he saw a movement on the opposite side of the space. Ducking down and gazing more intently, he could see a buck peacefully nibbling on freshly sprouted green leaves.

As softly and as quietly as he could manage to creep, the man moved forward, knowing that the crack of a single twig or branch beneath him could send the deer bolting away into the trees. Slowly, he bent his knees and aimed his rifle at the creature, his left eye pinched shut as his right eye squinted over the top of the weapon. One pull of the trigger now, would grant him his wish of catching a deer. But as he gazed, he realized how valuable the deer's life was to all of nature, and how delicate its fragile body seemed. It wouldn't be fair to kill it. Thoughtfully, the man tucked the pistol back under his arm. After one last look at the buck, still eating on the other side of the clearing, he turned and began to hike back through the forest towards home.

Not a mistake in sight. But even more noteworthy is the mood. The clear, pictorial sentences, the detailed vocabulary, the syntax and cadence which result from conscious transitions and adherence to our Avoid List. As we saw, the writer wanted to become a computer programmer, already was a computer programmer. He had no literary aspirations. What will it mean to him thirty years from now that he once wrote such a story? Judging by the eloquent responses I received from two former students, both now 50 years old, both successful in the sciences, it will mean a lot.

Forty years ago, long before I had honed the concept of pictorial writing to the point presented in these pages, I shepherded my class of 7th and then 8th graders through a rigorous program of writing. "A Moment on a Mountain Stream" on page 50 by James came from that class. So does the story below by David, a Waldorf "lifer" (Rudolf Steiner School, NYC, Class of 1984), now a physician with impressive titles (he agreed to being identified).

David Slotwiner, MD, FACC, FHRS
Chief, Division of Cardiology; Electrophysiology
New York Presbyterian Hospital Queens
Assistant Professor of Medicine
Weill Cornell Medical College
School of Health Policy and Research

David's Story

A Hard Days [sic] Night?

[The title was very lightly penciled in, and the question mark meant the writer wasn't sure it was a good title.]

Dew sparkled on the lush green grass. The first rays just peeped over the silloueted *[sic]* hills. As the sun rose slightly higher, and all the grass sparkled, the first bird started to sing. Then a robin flew down from a tree where it was perched and started seeking for worms in the ground. Just as the robin got a worm out of the ground, a blue jay came and snatched it away. The robin cried but could do nothing, so she went on to look for new food. As the sun grew higher in the sky, more and more birds came out to look for food. The dew began to evaporate and the katydids and crickets started singing, telling the world it would be a hot day.

In the distance, a father and son could just be distinguished between the swaying wheat and barely *[sic]* stalks. As they neared, one could see they were on a tractor heading out for a day's work. The father was dressed in an old, patched-up pair of jeans and a red plaid shirt. He wore boots and and *[sic]* a blue bandana that looked as though it had not been washed in many weeks. His face was dirty and there was a scar on his right arm. His limbs looked strong.

They could probably lift the front of a small car. The son's jeans were very dirty, and had holes at the knees. He wore a blue, oil-stained shirt, heavy work shoes and a red cap. His hair was neatly combed. His face was small and pale. He looked rather strong too, but maybe a bit lazy. He was sitting in the back of the tractor sucking on a piece of grass, staring into the tractor. They had a basket with their lunch in it so they could eat in the field, and work the whole day.

As they neared their destination, the tractor slowed down. The tractor came to a halt at the edge of the forest, just where the field ended. The boy hopped out and they prepared to fell the larg [sic] oak tree. They boy asked his father, "Do ya' wana use the big saw or the little on [sic]."

"I think we'll use the big one." said the father. They began to saw. As they sawed the tree, on could hear the swoosh-swoosh, swoosh-swoosh of the razor sharp blade cutting against the hard wood. The dull monotones [sic] sound dragged on all day, and by the end of the day, they had filled up the whole trailer.

The last rays of the sun slowly disappeared over the mountain. A cool breeze blew through the trees as the first bat flew overhead. The two workers decided it was time to start heading back. The eavening [sic] star was just visible as they shut the gate behind them, they turned and looked back at the work they had done, and with an inner pride, they latched the gate.

David's father was a doctor. He had four sons, all at the Rudolf Steiner School, and David was the oldest. I remember David's dad very well. At my first meeting with the parents of the class I would take on in 7th grade (which had had three previous class teachers), David's father pitched a fast ball at me: "What makes you think you can handle this class?" he challenged. Luckily I was young and naïve enough to think that having spent five years as a high school teacher had prepared me, and that's what I said. A few months later, the dad came in for a parent meeting (there was a very active and engaged mom in the picture, but it's the dad I need to focus on for our story here), and expressed concern that his oldest son was just not going to measure up. How would he ever get on in high school, let alone college? I assured him that David was a wonderful human being. I told the worried dad that during rehearsals of our recent class play, David had been at my side even before I needed something, a prop or a broom, or a chair. I assured him that David was a bit dreamy perhaps, but was observant, kind and considerate, and always on an even keel. I could imagine him as a fine nurse or possibly a psychologist, I told the doctor dad.

Little did I imagine that David, almost 40 years later, would be not just a highly regarded cardiologist, but an active advocate of patient rights, especially in the realm of electronic implants.

I found David through the internet, and we connected by phone. That was amazing! Then we scheduled a follow-up conversation into his busy week. He told me about himself, his career, his family, his awakened interest in writing, of which he now does a lot as he submits proposals and reports. Both of us, the former teacher and the former student, were deeply moved by the unexpected warmth and familiarity after all these years.

Was his culminating 8th grade story prescient? Indeed it was. Look at the tenderness with which he observes the animals, the social awareness with which he presents the characters, the harmony and organic wholeness of the story.

In response to my request to send me a few words about what he remembered of our work together from that time and the role writing played in his subsequent studies and career, David sent the following. I include it in its entirety because it is (a) a good piece of writing and (b) such a wonderful tribute to Waldorf education.

Learning to read did not come easily to me. By second grade and especially third grade, it became clear that I was behind my peers. This worried me because I knew it would interfere with my life objective—formed in kindergarten as one of my earliest memories—to follow my father's footsteps and become a physician. Every night my father would come home as my mother was putting my brothers and me to sleep. If my brother Peter and I were lucky, we would be allowed to stand in the kitchen and listen to my father recount stories from the day: Diagnosing a patient who had been misdiagnosed 3 years by a series of inferior physicians, relieving suffering and pain, and his stories of profusely grateful patients and families and respect from his colleagues. It seemed clear to me even at that very early age that there could be no more respected course than a career in medicine. Of course now I have a more sober perspective. But at that young age I realized—as did my father—that learning to read was going to be a deal breaker.

Desperate for advice, my parents met with Henry Barnes, the principal of the Rudolf Steiner school at that time. He advised my father to spend 30 minutes with me reading out loud each night. This was no small request since it meant significantly altering his schedule. For reasons I do not know, Henry Barnes suggested we repeat the *Lion, the Witch and the Wardrobe* by C.S. Lewis—one of the few books I dislike to this day. But Henry Barnes's advice worked: By the end of the year I had caught up to my peers and had mastered the skill of reading with one important caveat: I read slowly, focusing on each word.

With the skill of reading now under my belt, I quickly discovered books to be portals which would unlock my imagination. I spent one summer living as Pip, in *Great Expectations*, entranced by the roller coaster world created by Charles Dickens. Between 6th and 8th grades I read every book written by John Steinbeck and Ernest Hemingway. And so when it came time in 7th and 8th grades to put pen to paper, I had many ideas, raw emotions, and beliefs flowing through my mind. But I quickly learned that without structure I was unable to convey these thoughts and emotions to the reader.

My memory of learning to write during 7th and 8th grades is primarily learning the importance of the arc of the narrative. How to begin, develop and conclude the story, and how to structure each paragraph both within itself and in relation to the entire story. Reading my story from that time reminds me of my focus on creating this arc. The story has a clear beginning (morning), middle (afternoon) and end (night). But I also recognize my struggle to create imagery and atmosphere for the reader by using vocabulary and syntax that did not come naturally to me.

During high school my appreciation of literature grew, as did my appreciation for the art and craft of writing. But I was primarily focused on my goal of becoming a physician. Biology, chemistry and physics were my areas of focus. At Steiner, with Ekkehard Piening as my advisor, reading and writing were always important. But I expected these would be quickly left behind once I graduated from Steiner and began to pursue my career in medicine. I also recall clearly several classmates whose abilities to write engaging and insightful and often amusing essays always amazed and impressed me. They were the writers. I did not anticipate needing or wanting to develop my writing skills in the future.

The University of Chicago turned out to be about as opposite from Rudolf Steiner as one could imagine. The pedagogy emphasized the scientific method, competition amongst students, and grading on a strict bell curve where C was the average. Yet there was one strong similarity with Steiner: the emphasis on a broad liberal arts education. As I struggled to keep up in my science classes, I was also drawn to the most challenging and selective creative writing classes. There was no academic need or advantage for me to take these small, selective seminar classes on creative writing. They added enormous burdens of work (both reading and writing) to my already heavy science course load which I needed for a biology major. At most universities this work would have been recognized with a minor degree. But the University of Chicago, true to form, did not believe in awarding minor degrees.

I cannot recall if I stopped to ask myself why I was subjecting myself to these extremely challenging courses when I could barely keep up with my science classes. I can imagine what I would have said at the time: These books and essays are windows to studying the human condition which fulfilled a need that I was not receiving from my science classes. In my mind, these linked perfectly with my goal of becoming a physician: biology to study the art and science of medicine, literature and writing to understand the human condition and the individuals I would encounter as a physician. The great books I was reading and the wonderful professors who led the courses were unlocking centuries of human experiences, thought and wisdom. I felt stimulated by the exposure to these ideas, professors, my classmates and the discussions. The overwhelming point I took away both from reading and writing in college was that every word matters. The writer may not even be fully aware of his or her intentions by choosing a specific word—but it was chosen for a reason. I found this concept incredibly stimulating and provocative.

When I entered medical school, writing and playing music (another passion of mine) took a back seat. The first two years of medical school are spent in classrooms, much like college, but with a more intense workload. As with my other science classes, I found the first two years of medical school difficult. When we got to our clinical rotations in the third year, it was a whirlwind of experiences. The year was divided into rotations on the surgical, internal medicine, pediatrics, obstetrics and gynecology and psychiatry services. Somewhere during this year, we were supposed to decide what we wanted to be when we grew up. I chose my specialty (internal medicine) for the same reason most of my peers chose theirs: because I identified most closely with the values, priorities and personalities of physicians in this discipline.

After medical school the real education began. Internship and residency, 36-hour work shifts, being responsible for patients my own age who are dying of AIDS, breast cancer or leukemia. It had absolutely nothing to do with anything I had learned in college or medical school. It had everything to do with listening to patients, families, attending physicians who taught me that trade craft of medicine, listening to nurses, pharmacists and housekeepers. All of these people knew more about healthcare than I did. By listening to each of these experts and working as hard as I could to understand their perspective, I realized I had finally found my calling. At every previous stage of my education, I had struggled and had been an outsider. But this came naturally to me, and I excelled.

As I became more confident, after completing training, I began to seek out avenues to improve some of the many problems with our healthcare delivery system. A few topics quickly rose to the top of my agenda. I was appalled at the conflict of interest created by a fee-for-service incentive structure that encourages physicians and the healthcare system to perform often unnecessary tests and procedures. I was also shocked by the limited ability of regulatory agencies to monitor the performance of medical devices once they were approved and released into the general medical practice. Unexpectedly, my skills as a writer have found a new role and voice as I have gravitated towards health policy issues and as I seek avenues to change and improve our delivery of healthcare. The narrative arc, the attention to each word, and the importance of swaying the reader now have greater significance for me than I could have ever imagined.

Clearly, our former middle schoolers do write on! and then some.

David and James—the two little boys for whom reading did not come easily, but who, by the time I taught them in their 7th and 8th grade years, were appreciative readers and able writers—both went on to excel in their chosen fields in the sciences and continue to find value in their relationship to language. How could I ever have guessed, when I chose—goodness knows why—their 8th grade stories to file away, that 40 years later their stories and the men they now are would surface like this?

To Continue

For several years now, I've included a final composition as part of the 8th grade "Block Review" or final test. The students know it's coming. Part I of the test concerns our confusing words and punctuation for quotations. Part II is a short story. Part III consists of questions about our reading. For Part II, the heart of the test, I provide a context, as I have in all previous story writing assignments. My instructions might look like this:

> Write a story (IN INK, SKIPPING LINES)
> Setting: Along the coast or at a beach
> Character(s): A nature photographer and his/her dog
> Don't forget to include a turning point.
> Start by making a brief outline.
> EDIT YOUR OWN WORK

I allow about 50 minutes for the story. I let the students know that the story is worth 55% of the overall grade for the final test.

By now, the task of writing a composition on demand is familiar; we've written about two a week for the past three weeks. With that much practice, it can be done even as part of a test, where time is limited.

Because creativity on demand might seem too difficult, I'll include some of the results. The first is by a girl who struggled mightily with the technicalities of spelling, grammar and punctuation. She was particularly young in her bearing and outlook, and still a bit sleepy in her grasp of details. Yet, somehow, the constraints of the test invigorated her:

My Story

[Well, at least it is "My" story and not "A" story. She was one of the few to attempt the indicated outline, but stopped mid-word.]

Outline of my character:
Has brown hair and hazle colored eyes.
She is wearing fr

Waves crash along the clear yellow sand. *[She has picked up on the idea of not beginning each sentence with "The."]* The clear water *[By the second sentence she is back to the usual syntax, starting with "The."]* pulls rock *[sic]* with it every time it crashs. four paws splash thew the waves as a large yellow golden *[Labrador Retriever]* rushes up the beach glad to be free of his lesh. behind the happy dog walks a women dressed in a pair of rolled up jeans and a zip up jacket. *[She has learned to add a detail about the character.]* The woman also careys a small camera around her neck.

Sitting on a large rock near the water the woman starts to look for a good shot of the water crashing on the shore. *[nice! a good place to position the character with her camera]* At just the right mount she snaps *[indecipherable word, perhaps "several"]* shots before moving down the beach for the best shot of the setting sun over the water. *[A more sophisticated writer might have avoided repeating "shot."]* After the women toke many more shots she begins to call her dog back so they can leave. *[Vague. She is not really seeing this in her mind's eye, but to her credit, she realizes that she needs to get the character off the beach.]* When the golden runs to her owner the dog has a large pice of drift wood in her mouth and waves back and forth. *[Okay. It's a good idea.]* The women reacher for the drift wood to throw it back in to the water, but as she grabs it something catchs her eyes *[Ah!]* Small wave like water patterns line the base of the log. *[The pivotal sentence, with its unique detail, is completely correct.]* Smiling the woman takes out her camera and begins to take photos of the drift wood. After doing so the women begins to run down the beach to were the dog found the would. The women knew that the wood was very good for burning but the could have never got it was so pretty. *[Now our writer is so engaged in the action, that the words tumble onto the paper somewhat chaotically.]*

After a long day at the beach the woman and her dog make there way back home this time with lots of photos and a new mistory. When later checking her photos the women finds that the wave pattern is from the drift wood being lost in the water and wearing it slowly over time down. *[Hmmm, not sure really what is happening, but what a wonderfully artistic sensibility to focus on the pattern of the wood on the sand, to be aware of the incoming tide]*

As her teacher, I was thrilled by her effort. My comment on her test commends her for a good story and a good job of describing the setting and characters even though, as I also let her know, the spelling and punctuation are at a ✓- (check minus) level. Although this girl is so young in many ways, and not yet fully awake intellectually, she often met me with a level and discerning gaze, which she also cast upon the hijinks of her fellow 8th graders. Luckily, her parents have not undermined her self-esteem by harping on her poor spelling. To judge by her older sister, who suffered similar orthographic tumult as an 8th grader, and is now a successful college student, the "driftwood writer" will overcome the confusion she now spills onto the paper and keep the discerning eye and fundamental levelheadedness. I'd bet on it.

Our next example of a story written as part of the final test comes from an able writer with a strong imagination and a very slow, dreamy pace. She took her time over each assignment.

Camera Catastrophe

Far below the rocky cliff is a secret beach. *[The verb is "is"—the student crossed out "lies"—let's see where this goes.]* The rising water pounds the shore, creating an outline on the sand. *[Sentence starts with "The," which, as we know by now, is not the best idea. "Creating an outline on the sand" is a good image, but would there be an outline if the surf is pounding?]* Several elephant seals try to waddle to the dry part of the beach. *["Dry" is good as contrast/transition to the rising water of previous sentence.]*

A car door can be heard echoing against the craggy rocks. Soon a young women steps onto the treacherous trail leading down from the road *[from where]* she parked her car on to the beach. Her chestnut colored hair is tyed back in a ponytail, so the ferocious coast winds don't blow it in her face. She is wearing jeans, boots, and a black parka in order to stay warm. *[The writer has attended to the description of the character. She doesn't quite trust the picture and adds information to both descriptive sentences: "so the ferocious winds don't blow it in her face" and "in order to stay warm."]* Hanging from a strap on her shoulder is a brand new camera. *[We know there has to be a camera, and here it is, almost a part of her clothing.]*

As she continues down the path a root juts up in front of her. *[Had our writer included plants with roots in the initial*

*reference to the path, instead of just calling it "treacherous,"
this root would not be mere convenience.]* Without seeing it
[She means "Not seeing it."], she accidently catches her foot
and falls to the ground. Her camera stap *[sic]* comes loose,
and falls off her shoulder onto the ground *[repeated word]*
ahead of her. Dusting off her clothes the young women
struggles to regain her balance. *[Would she be dusting off her
clothes if she were actually struggling to regain her balance?
Probably the writer meant that the character dusted off her
clothes as she stood up.]* When she sees the camera on the
ground she hastily grabs it to check the damage. Slowly she
turns it over to see *[look at]* the lens and sees a tiny crack
that had *[has]* spread over the unprotected *[good]* glass. "Oh
no!" she sobs, as she heads back up the hill. She had broken
her brand new camera, and did not have enough money to
buy a new one. She took one last look at the elephant seals
on the beach below, and drove off in her car. *[the quick
ending probably due to lack of time.]*

Our writer ran out of time. The photographer didn't get far. To
finish this story, the writer would have needed not only more time,
but many rewrites, to correct the small inaccuracies she doesn't
notice while in the throes of writing.

This girl's written work had a wonderful streak of originality.
She simply didn't take well to the confines of time. In her paragraph
about herself, she wrote:

Hello, my name is <u>first name</u> <u>last name</u>. I am 14 years old
and in the 8th grade at _____ Waldorf School. Outside of
school I enjoy reading, singing, acting, drawing and dance.
At school I am currently working on my 8th grade project.

For my project I am researching theater and costume design, and designing costumes for different plays.

I hope that in high school I can learn in an engaging way. I also hope I can continue pursuing my passions outside of school.

I hope to get into Stanford, the New School at NYU, the Royal School of Drama, or Rhode Island School of Design (RISD), and I hope I can exel [sic] at my classes if I go there. I would love to be a director for plays or movies, or a singer once I finish my senior year of college.

Singing, acting, drawing and dance, and... reading. She is 14, and she feels herself to be an artist, a creative person, a person who wants to design costumes, or possibly (ambitiously) to direct plays or movies. The real and perceptible is mixed in with lofty, almost unattainable hopes and ambitions. So her piece about the woman photographer on the beach is clearly perceived, but not so clearly executed. In summoning up the details about the woman, our writer has completely forgotten the dog. Given more time, she would most certainly have arrived at a quaint and original portrait of the dog, seen through the lens of her own unique imagination.

To conclude our examples of command performance stories, here is one by a young lady, an 8th grader, who crossed out but did not obliterate the following sentence in her "Paragraph About Myself":

I can't wait to leave Waldorf and go to a high school where people appreciate me for who I am not who they want me to be. I will work hard and make friends.

The conspicuously legible crossed-out sentence follows upon:

> I am currently attending _____ Waldorf School. My
> hobbies consist of Musical Theater, Singing Lessons. I do
> TRX, Crossfit, Spin and Yoga. I like to make cards. I like to
> fashion design and talking.

After the crossing out, she continues:

> I love to do nothing more than travel. I plan to have a ton
> of adventures with my friends and travel the world. I love
> musical and New York City. I enjoy healthy eating, getting
> work done, weekends, kiwis, vacations and laughing with
> people until my stomach hurts. *[This sequence of things she
> enjoys is excellent for its innovative approach to a list. It has a
> journalistic ring to it.]* I like places where everything is clean
> and organized NOT CLUTTERED!
>   In high school I will work hard and make friends who
> appreciate me for who I am and not who they want me
> to be. *[Perhaps it was when she wrote this again that she
> scratched out the first mention of it.]* My best friends are…
> *[She mentions nine names.]*

She talks about her sister who is her "best friend." Then continues:

> I enjoy making weird *[spelled correctly!]* snap chats with
> her *[the sister]* and laughing about stuff other people won't
> understand. After high school I want to travel, and be happy
> and make money and laugh all the time.

This student pushed the envelope at every opportunity. When
she flounced into class with a cup of some drink in a large paper

cup (Starbucks type) and I told her she couldn't have that in class, she became combative. We compromised that she could keep it at her desk but not drink from it. Later of course I learned from the regular teacher that it was against the rules to bring cups like that into class. She came late. She missed class. She didn't participate in our opening verse, clamping her mouth shut. She passed notes, or tried to. She exuded enormous boredom. BUT: she was a natural writer and a good student and in spite of herself; she found her hand shooting up to answer questions even when she was doing her best to be obstreperous. The character in her photographer-on-the-beach story is "I." Hers was the only first-person narrative offered during that test.

The Linearen Parrott.

Clear watered waves gently lap up agenst the white sand, reflecting the color of the strikingly blue summer sky. Across from the water, on the other side of the long beach, palm trees strech their fruit full limbs in every direction, the bottom palms sagging from the weight of young coconuts. *["Clear-watered waves" and "fruit-full limbs" are poetic phrases. They tell me that the writer is looking for a personal way to describe the scene. Those phrases, and the palms sagging under the weight of the coconuts, impressed themselves on the writer's memory.]*

Glancing down at my tan toes, barely submerged in the cool water *[ambivalent punctuation—Are the toes or the character barely submerged?]*, I notice a small cream colored shell just poking out from under the smooth sand. *[It doesn't take long for the first person narrator to enter the scene.]* I sink to one knee to get a closer look. Speckled with flecks of coral and green, the shell *[She has crossed out "seems like it"—she remembered to avoid "seems"]* would be perfect for an underwater shot *[a very good transition: from the shell, which is a very organic catalyst in this setting, to the camera].* Pulling my large "Canon IQ" camera from by my side, I remove the lense and apply to blue "(u)h2O" Lense and snap a shot of the tiny shell. Once I have a good photo, *[She is so filled with the character's actions, that it doesn't occur to her to provide a description of the "good" photo.]* I sling my camera back by my side, grab the shell and head back twards my towel and bags under the swaying palm trees. Setting my camera back in her leather case, I see a ripe mango, fallen from a near by tree. I rip it open with my teeth *[!],* I begin to ponder why I am here. *[another good transition, though probably the character was lying back on the sand chewing on the juicy mango while ruminating on why she was here.]* The "Aplicant Letter" I recieved *[sic]* from Cal, four days ago says to create a portfolio that tells "who you are". I am Hawaiian, I am authentic, I am strong… I guess Im beautiful. *[Yes, she really is authentic and strong, and the modesty of the "I guess" is unexpected and welcome.]* All of the photos I have taken of the water, sunrise, small shells and palm trees have shown who I am, I guess, *[Would a "strong" person be so diffident? Possibly, though perhaps some lack of confidence is poking through.]* but Im not sure I have the ground breaking photo *[a mature and experienced insight here].* I need a star of the show. As I wipe the sweet mango juice off of my mouth, I whistle for my old, loving hound Mahalio *[Hmmm. Mahalio is "convenient" bounding into the story out of nowhere. She ought to have been introduced earlier.]* Mahalio comes bounding up, her blonde fur sticking up like a por-e-pine's, from the salty water. She nuzzles into my side as I lean back onto my warm towel.

Eyes closed, I begin to doze; dreaming of all of the striking photos the other seniors in high school, trying to get into Call will present. My light and cottony *[nice!]* dreams are harshly intturupted by a loud "caw"ing sound, coming from the sky. I sit bolt upward, one hand one Mahalio and one hand over my racing heart. Looking up frantically, my blue eyes catch the source of the cawing sound. With that, a great Linearen Parrot comes swooping down from the mango tree above me. Hawaiian, authentic, strong, <u>really</u> beautiful *[Wow! She has a parrot who is a real metaphor for herself, that's quite sophisticated.]*... the words race through my mind as I scramble to grab my camera. Clicking the off/on switch I focus, zoom then shoot! Shoot again! The Camera clicks away as I squint my eyes, trying to catch the stop motion. Then the linear is gone, the bright yellow bird of parddise is no longer here, leaving me with nothing but those frantic photos *[not sure what she means, but it works]* and the echo of its taunting *[great word]* call.

Six months later the letter of acceptance is in my mail box, explaining the smile provokingly news.

I couldn't find "Linearen Parrot" on the internet, but, as I commented on this girl's paper, "Is there such a thing as a Linearen Parrot? Not that it matters." I limited my comment to: "Authentic and well-executed." I did not include any of the bracketed comments I've inserted here. She got a ✓+ and that was my only other comment. In this composition, she dropped her antagonistic mask long enough to do a really good job. True, the spelling is an issue, but that's not what the story or the main lesson block was about.

8TH GRADE

CREATIVE

WRITING

WITH MISS WINTER

DECEMBER
2015

Organizing that Flurry of Papers

So far we've talked about possible content for this course. Let's look at how to keep track of the paper tide. Organization is key.

I prefer to have the students use 1-inch wide, 3-hole punch binders with side pockets. On the first day of class, each student has 5 dividers, and we name them:

1. Table of Contents
2. Work
3. Notes
4. Final Copies
5. Literature

Naturally, the "Work" section will be the biggest, and to avoid endless confusion and argument, each exercise and each piece of writing, whether class work or homework, is dated and numbered. I ask a secretarial type to be our secretary and to keep track. It's the secretary's task to keep track for the entire class, and the list of exercises and assignments, which includes date due, title, and assigned number, is a public document, up on the board or wall. I specify that we are keeping our sections chronological by date with the most recent work at the front of the section. It takes frequent reminders to get into the habit, but once a student has received a ✓- (check minus) (more on this below) because of a missing date or no number for the assignment, it becomes easier to remember to label each piece of paper in the Work section.

Homework due today should be in the front pocket of the binder. Returned work that needs to be corrected should be in the back pocket. Having watched students spend seven minutes rifling through their binders for work due, I've concluded that the logistical challenge must be met with clear and precise instructions.

Although we do not amass great quantities of "Notes," it is useful to isolate them in their own section. Our Avoid List, for example, would be in the Notes section, as would be our notes on punctuation of quotation marks, or our Confusing Words.

"Final Copies" are rarely required, because our emphasis is on improving and correcting drafts, and it is the content rather than the appearance of the paper we're concerned with. Nevertheless, I try to make sure that there is at least one complete story that is copied over, preferably on unlined paper, possibly illustrated, and placed in its special section. (For a brief consideration of handwriting vs. keyboard, see page 178.)

The "Literature" section is where our photocopied short stories are filed. In California, where most of the 8th grades I've taught were located, I often used either "Dutch Courage," or "The Banks of the Sacramento," both short stories by Jack London. It's useful to have one or two short stories at hand. For one thing, it allows for some reading and comprehension work, which provides a good change of pace from the writing. For another, having students read aloud always lowers the barometric pressure in a classroom. Then, too, reading established writers allows questions about motives or character or alternative outcomes, which ought to be discussed so that we don't fall into reading by rote. We should be thinking about what we're reading. We should learn to appreciate an author's particular gift or agenda.

I have also used Hemingway's *Old Man and the Sea*, and there is much to be gained from it, especially the frequent similes, the precision and specificity of the descriptions, the masterful characterizations of the old man and the boy. On the final test (more on that later), I usually asked the students to tell me whether they thought the story ended positively or negatively, and I found that most of them thought the old man won the fight, even though he came home defeated by the sharks.

Over the years, I've felt less and less happy about this choice of reading material. Neither Hemingway's prose nor the depiction of struggle—the old man's and the marlin's—seemed appropriate for 8th graders. And their written responses to questions about the story testify to their general lack of real understanding for the content. It's about the right length, though, and it does captivate the young people. Surely there is a better alternative, and I hope you find it.

Tracking and Evaluating Every Single Assignment

My credibility as a teacher is facilitated when the students know that I take their work seriously. To that end, I keep track of every assignment, have a comment, even if it's only "Good work!" on every assignment, and check their binders at the end of the course, if not before, to ensure that each and every exercise is accounted for and corrected adequately.

One method I've used to manage this torrent of paper is simply to number every single exercise, whether it was done in class or at home. It's essential to have a continuous numbering system which includes all work. Each piece of work must have its own name, date and number and, of course, the student's name. And, as already mentioned, we have a designated Number Tracker, or secretary, to keep us on course for our Table of Contents.

The harder part is how to correct each student's work so that it can be returned the next day. When this can be managed, the flow from day to day becomes more organic. By seeing how they did yesterday, students are often motivated to improve for tomorrow. As every teacher knows, keeping track is a matter of organization. Sometimes you have to have a day without homework, just so that you can catch up. That might be a good day for assigning some reading.

Over the years I've developed a simple yet effective evaluation method. There is the ✓ (check) or the ✓- (check minus) or the ✓+ (check plus). Even for adults, I find that, vague as these categories are, they work, they motivate. The ✓ means it's okay. Nothing to write home about, but not bad. The ✓- means it's not up to snuff, below par. Perhaps it was illegible, or it was the wrong task. The ✓+ means it's above average, good job! I explain this system when I return the first set of homework papers. Simple as it sounds, the students get into it. They are eager for that check plus and are happy to see it. Most of the time, I'm dispensing the average ✓. The ✓+ means that something the student did deserves special commendation. A ✓+ inserted above a word or sentence or beside a paragraph can be a springboard for greater effort next time. A ✓+ can be encouraging for a middle-of-the-road student. The ✓- is rare. It means failure, and it is rarely justified. I do my best to avoid it, but I don't hesitate to use it when I feel it's pedagogical to do so.

I also track the late work (L), the incomplete work (INC), the work that needs to be done over (DO) because, say, the point of the task was missed entirely or the writing is illegible. These three assessments often give way to a happier appraisal, and so erasable pencil in my ledger is practical.

By the second week of the block, I might up the ante by awarding a letter grade. Whether I'm using letter grades or the check system when evaluating a story, I give two separate marks, as described earlier in the spelling section.

To encourage the poor spellers, who are often "fantasy rich"[25] and would love to write if only they wouldn't lose their footing so often on the spelling scree debris, I often evaluate the written work according to two separate criteria: technicalities and content. Technicalities includes spelling, grammar, and punctuation; content takes into account how well the task was executed and includes originality and depth. We shouldn't let technical problems obscure the student's intentions. It's not always the technically proficient student who gets to the heart of the story. When a struggling student is recognized for the *what* instead of the *how*, miracles happen.

Here, for example, is the unvarnished work of a young lady now a junior in college. She wrote this in 8th grade, in response to the "Harriet" assignment, which involved finishing a piece of writing for which I had provided the start:

> "Well hi, how are [sic] today?" said an unmisstakabley friendly voice in front of her. Wel of courarce this was her dearest Grandma. But it ook about 5 mintues to make her self belev it actually was her grandma. And when she did believe, she yelled "oh grandma how nice of you to come" but her tone of voice was srachy and coarce and did'nt at all sound friendly. But her grandma knew that Harriet did'nt mean to sound so bad it was just from her cold.

"Well when is your shift over" said grandma politely. "It ends in a 5 mintues" said Harriet. "So I can meet you in my car?" "Okay" says grandma. "Wow," thought Harriet, how nice of her to come.

"I did'nt exspect snow this early in december, said Harriet tring to start a comversation. "Yes, but not to early for us in Colorado, in fact, said Grandma, as she started the car. "Before the flight last night, I had to dig my car out of the snow. "No you did'nt Grandma," harriet said. "It does'ent even snow where you live in Colorado." "Sorry I just want to move back home in the mountains away from any evil doctors and people like that." But what if you got very ill? Who would save you?"

"Do you take the expressway or the bollivard to your house? I forget," said Grandma, trying to change the convesation. "The expressway groaned" Harriet.

What a mess! Yes, but under the clods are seeds waiting to bloom. Here is what this same girl wrote seven years later, in response to my request for any thoughts on that 8th grade course during which she wrote about Harriet and much more, all similarly heartfelt, all similarly clumsy:

Dear Dorit,

It is wonderful to hear from you. I am so grateful to be here and have this chance to explore Europe. Budapest is so quirky and lovely. It is also a part of a different side of Europe. A side that I hardly learned about in school. This component has made my visit extra special.

It is a trend amongst Americans students studying abroad to tour the various cities of Europe each weekend. I'm now in Rome for the second time. I'll go back tomorrow for Budapest.

Last weekend I had the pleasure of going to the Cycladic island of Paros and then to Athens. The island was so beautiful, and full of classic white buildings and very kind people. I came at the perfect time, because Budapest is completely in the fall and becoming darker with each day. It also wasn't exactly tourist season in Greece so we got the island, especially those pristine beaches, all to ourselves.

If there is anything I have learned from my trip so far is the huge importance of kindness, and acceptance both on my part and by of host country/cultures I visit.

To answer your questions…

Unfortunately I don't remember specifically writing these pieces, but I know the process of your class and the fundamentals of Waldorf education have massively impacted how I approach life. So I'll answer your questions through what I believe is the best way, remembering my high school writing experience.

In high school, freshman year especially, my classmates writing was noticeably different. They had mastered a straightforward, basic and practical technique that accommodated what the teachers expected. The shift in learning environments during the first year was traumatic. I sank deep to the level of the what the assignments expected. Many of the skills I had worked hard to develop in middle school, quickly deteriorated and I can remember thinking "I've forgotten how to write".

Flash-forward to my last year of HS, things really changed. This turn around could've been a result to a lot of factors. Now as a psychology student, I am aware of even more potential factors.

I took an AP level English class, and some honors classes. With this next period of adjustment, my creative writing past was reawakened. I quickly built off my previous developments in writing. When it came time to build the skills for reading, analyzing and picking apart texts that the AP test required, I felt extremely prepared.

Your class and maybe my even my entire Waldorf background helped me develop an intuition to ask why and to hunt for the answers in the unique or less obvious places.

Because of my specific past academic experiences, I find the strength in my writing and overall Waldorf influenced approach on life to be a serious advantage.

Spell-check can account for some of it, but here is the blossoming soul of an able student. To round out this particular picture, here is the narrative report I wrote at the time. Her letter grade for our course was a C:

_____'s writing has improved considerably since our last block together. Her spelling is better, as is her handwriting. She still struggles with these technicalities, but she is more fluent in her expression. She enjoys writing and has good ideas, but she can get distracted and go off on irrelevant, complicated tangents. In class _____ is now more able to concentrate on the topic at hand, but here too her attention is likely to wander. Reading aloud is something she needs to work on. Young in her story telling, she often has mature and helpful insights into her classmates' stories and the literature we read together. In sum, _____ is still below grade level in her writing, but the rate of improvement indicates that she *can* catch up.

And, indeed, her "mature and helpful insights into her classmates' stories" blossomed into the study of psychology. Her "level of writing" certainly did "catch up."

As we go up in the grades, by 7th, definitely by 8th, obviously more often by 9th, I do throw in more and more letter grades, especially for the longer stories. Often I give two letter grade evaluations, one for content, one for mechanics, i.e., grammar, spelling, punctuation. On any quizzes or on the final test, or block evaluation as it is sometimes euphemistically called, I provide letter grades for each section of the test and average them into an overall letter grade evaluation. It's important, though, also to include comments. The teacher's handwritten comments are personal, and the students appreciate that. You can acknowledge effort, or improvement, or other intangibles, or the need for more effort, or greater use of a dictionary, or more legible handwriting and so forth, when you put a personal comment on a student's work. A long time ago, when I was a class teacher, the mother of the most capable student in the class told me that my personal comments on the boy's compositions meant a great deal to him; he was used to excellent grades, but he valued my comments, which were very specific. I might, for example, point out that a particular sentence was really successful, or that a word could be improved. (The student, in fact, was James, the oceanographer we met earlier.)

In fact, challenging the better writers is often best achieved through written comments. Here is the recent response from another of those 8th graders I taught seven years ago. This lad was a very bright student. In retrospect, he finds himself less than flawless:

> I certainly feel that I was better prepared as a writer going in
> to high school than many of my friends from non-Waldorf
> schools. It is hard to say why exactly that was because it's hard
> to be introspective when you are 14, but I certainly think your
> classes had a lot to do with it. (Also, I was so arrogant at that time
> in my life that I'm sure it would have been impossible for me

to give anyone/anything credit for my success besides my own intelligence.) On that note though, I remember that class in 8th grade because it was one of the few times in middle school where I was told "good job, but do it again." There was a real emphasis on doing things differently and improving (such as the multiple tenses exercise). So often in school, it was just "great job [name]" and then we would move on.

[…]

I think that your class in 8th grade was maybe the first time when I had to actually come out and try again. That creative writing block was no doubt beneficial for my writing abilities, but more than that I think it was beneficial for my drive, ambition, and initiative. Those were the things I would need more than writing skills going into high school, and certainly into college.

So many of the writings that we did in that 8th grade creative writing block were changes or improvements on previous work. That is very different than anything else we had been doing up until then in school. This new style of doing work was beneficial in the long run because it planted the seed of the idea that you cannot do something poorly and escape it by moving on to the next task. In the creative writing block, even when I started a new project it was always with the old ones in the back of my mind. That is similar to how work is done in high school and college, not how work had previously been done in grade school.

Doing this type of work planted the seed of an idea: good work isn't about natural talent, it is about persistence, about adjusting, about trying again. I was resistant to that idea at first, but it has been reinforced time and time again in my life. Looking back, I think that the 8th grade creative writing block was my first encounter with that idea. Coming face to face with that reality, even briefly, before high school was beneficial because I was not blindsided when I got graduated and moved on to an environment where I actually had to prove myself again and was no longer cut slack because of my reputation as a good student.

On the note of college, my Waldorf friends and I often remark on how no one seems to know how to write when they begin freshman year. Every single person here at [excellent university] was top of their class, great test scores, great admission essays, etc. … but when they start here they write in this way where they use a lot of big words, construct eloquent sentences, and succeed in saying nothing. As a Waldorf student I sometimes have to adjust my writing style for the academic environment, but it is much easier to bend real content into a mold than jam substance into a perfectly crafted essay.

The arrogant boy has come a long way. His 8th grade writing was technically suave, even though his handwriting was lazy. Beneath his façade of sophisticated indifference, his writing revealed the maturity and depth, which now as a junior in college, he articulates.

Most teachers, even those with experience, have such loaded plates that it's difficult for them to envision their students in the future. Therefore these reflections by former students are valuable reminders that eventually the work we do in the classroom is absorbed and transformed, metabolized so to speak, to become the future. Although the following comments do not have the sagacity of time passed, they nevertheless give us insights into how our efforts "arrived."

"What Did You Enjoy Most in This Course?"

Note: The language in all these examples has been corrected.

> *Student A:* I enjoyed learning about the different aspects of a short story and what makes a good short story. This was new to me so I found it very captivating. (overall ✓ + male student)

> *Student B:* My favorite part of the block was writing the stories. It was really fun for me. (overall ✓ - male student)

> *Student C:* My favorite part of the main lesson was listening to other people's stories, seeing what they did with the theme or first sentence. For me, reading someone's writing is like seeing a deeper, more private part of them that they don't realize is woven into their story. Seeing the amazing writers in this class has inspired me greatly. (overall ✓ + female student)

> *Student D:* My favorite part of the main lesson was listening to the creative writings my classmates came up with and getting inspired. I loved discussing the writings in class. (overall ✓ + male student)

> *Student E:* Before this block I had never been taught how to write properly! [exclamation added] and had never written fiction before, but the biggest thing I learned was probably to use transitions. (overall ✓ female student)

> *Student F:* My favorite part of the lessons was when we got to write settings, or characters, or stories or read each other's stories. The actual writing and/or listening to others was by far the best part of our main lesson and I enjoyed it immensely. (overall ✓ female student)

> *Student G:* I really like just being able to write everyday and learning new things. (overall ✓ + female student)

"What Did You Learn from This Course?"

Student A: I think the main thing I learned was about the characterization of characters and how that adds to the short story. (overall ✓ + male student)

Student B: I learned how to use vocabulary to make my stories better. (overall ✓ - male student)

Student C: I learned a great deal during this block. I grew in so many ways as a writer. I have better grammar, better punctuation… (overall ✓ + female student)

Student D: I think I learned the most about painting a picture with words. When we did the eucalyptus grove exercise, I realized how much better my writing sounded when I could visualize the scene. I cannot wait to apply this technique to my other school studies. (overall ✓ + male student)

Student F: I learned a lot during our lessons. I learned how to be a good writer: how to make characters come alive and my settings seemed real. I learned many tips on how to write a story and how to replace generic words to make my sentences better. (overall ✓ female student)

Student G: One thing that I hadn't really thought about in writing was the transitions. I think that when I was consciously thinking about them, it really improved my writing. (overall ✓ + female student)

Student H: I learned many things during this Main Lesson, but two things stick out. One of the things was emphasis on transitions. I had never really thought of them before, and polishing them has made my writing better. The second thing I learned was describing with nouns. Before this, I had never thought of it, and it too has helped me. (overall ✓ – male student)

Handwriting

The question of computer use often comes up. So far, all my teaching, even as recently as last spring (2016) has taken place in grade schools which don't permit keyboard-generated homework (unless for a very special project). But when the question comes to me, because students are hoping that a guest teacher has different rules, I am emphatic about the need for legible, double-spaced, handwritten work. Every page needs to have the student's name, the number of the assignment or exercise, and today's date, as well as a title. I explain that when you are looking for a job, your handwriting matters. I refer to recent articles (albeit online) on the importance, benefits and advantages of cursive writing.

There's lots of talk these days about whether anyone really needs to write by hand anymore. It's not a losing battle. Mainstream education, conventional wisdom, even neuroscience have recognized the positive results of writing by hand. Here's an excerpt from a *New York Times* article.

> Psychologists and neuroscientists say it is far too soon
> to declare handwriting a relic of the past. New evidence
> suggests that the links between handwriting and broader
> educational development run deep. Children not only learn
> to read more quickly when they first learn to write by hand,
> but they also remain better able to generate ideas and retain
> information.[26]

If you Google "Importance of Learning Cursive," you will find a whole bookcase of articles telling us why one of the basics of Waldorf education has been scientifically proven to be beneficial for the development not only of the child's brain, but also the child's capacity for learning. To wit:

> Studies illustrate how writing by hand engages the brain in learning. Recent studies suggest there is a big reason to maintain and learn this skill, which some people call a gift. Recently at Indiana University, researchers ... discovered that children's neural activity was far more enhanced when they practiced writing by hand after receiving instruction than when they simply looked at letters. "It seems there is something really important about manually manipulating and drawing out two-dimensional things we see all the time," says Karin Harman James, the assistant professor of psychology and neuroscience who led the study.[27]

> Contrary to the view that handwriting is a trivial skill, handwriting actually is important for a number of reasons. One involves the concept of mental resources to which I have alluded in several other columns, in relation to reading and mathematics as well as writing. Just as effortful word decoding may impair reading comprehension, or lack of automatic recall may reduce the mental resources available for learning advanced computational algorithms in math, labored handwriting creates a drain on mental resources needed for higher-level aspects of writing, such as attention to content, elaboration of details, and organization of ideas.
> Because handwriting is a basic tool used in many subjects—taking notes, taking tests, and doing classroom work and homework for almost every content area as well

as in language arts classes—poor handwriting can have a pervasive effect on school performance.

Moreover, when handwriting is perceived as arduous and time-consuming, motivation to write may be greatly reduced, leading to a lack of practice that may further compound difficulties with writing.[28]

Putting pen to paper stimulates the brain like nothing else, even in this age of e-mails, texts and tweets. In fact, learning to write in cursive is shown to improve brain development in the areas of thinking, language and working memory. Cursive handwriting stimulates brain synapses and synchronicity between the left and right hemispheres, something absent from printing and typing.[29]

So: when 8th graders groan about having to write by hand, I throw out some of the impressively researched scientific data at them. I also tell them that that's how I want it because it reminds me, as I read their work, of whose work I'm reading. So: it has to be legible. I am emphatic about the need for legible, double-spaced, handwritten work. Illegible work is unacceptable. If I have to puzzle over whether an "e" or an "i" is meant, the paper has to be rewritten. That's just common sense. When the student skips lines, it's easier for me to insert corrections. When it's handwritten, there's a personal connection between me and the writer, which makes my evaluation more relevant. My requests are not gratuitous. I can explain them. I find that when I insist on some formality—a real title, not just "Homework" and the date the assignment is due, as well as the number of the assignment and the student's name—it helps with the overall concept that how the page looks does matter. That gives the handwriting question a context.

Corrections

The bane of the English teacher's professional responsibility is the never-ending, torrent of corrections. Just as the math teacher would be leaving her job incomplete if she left wrong answers unattended, so the English teacher needs to point out the mistakes, and then, arduously, make sure the student has noticed. By English teacher, I really mean any teacher asking students to write. That would include the physics teacher and handwork teacher. Unfortunately, it falls to the main lesson teacher, or the English teacher per se, to follow through by seeing to it that mistakes don't get left unattended. Over the years I've developed some simple rules.

16 *Rule Number Sixteen:*
Do not let any piece of class work or homework
get thrown out.

Perhaps this should be Rule Number One. When students know that EVERYTHING they do for this course has value, that NOTHING will be discarded, they take their work more seriously, whether that's homework or class work. Rough drafts have as much value as polished final copies. Just as the math teacher will say, "Show your work, your process," so the teacher dealing with written language ought to explain that working through various stages, from draft to draft, is part of the craft of writing. It's good to keep the rough drafts near the final copy, so that you can make sure (even if only on a spot-check basis) that mistakes have been corrected.

17 Rule Number Seventeen: Do not let any class work or homework go uncorrected.

Yes, it's a lot of work for the teacher, but once you've established that you mean it, you don't need to collect the corrections (with the originals of course) 100% of the time. Sometimes you can just walk through the class, ledger in hand, to see whether corrections have been done. Perhaps you can collect the binders once a week. That way you won't be overwhelmed at the end of the block, though that is the time to be detailed in your assessment of whether corrections have been carried out 100%.

In my assignment-tracking ledger, I designate two columns for each task I've given the students, whether as class work or homework. One column tracks whether they did the work and how they did it. The second column tracks whether the item has been satisfactorily corrected. Notice: "satisfactorily."

Part of the reason that corrections become such a snarl is that there is no end to a slothful student's ingenuity for avoiding them. The realm of corrections is really a battle of wills. Either the teacher has enough will, or the student slips through the net.

So: I do my best to return each and every assignment the next day, and part of that day's homework is to correct the assignment returned today. The quick turnaround helps the students develop the habit of corrections. If, at every moment, I know who is behind in handing in either assignments or corrections, I can more swiftly address the issue with the student.

An effective measure to manage the ebb and flow of incoming and outgoing paper is a public tracker. By that I mean a chart on the wall with a row for each student's name and a column for each assignment and each correction. On this public chart you needn't include the actual grade (if you are giving grades) but simply use the same check mark to denote that the work was done. When there is an epidemic of late work, I take the time to put a little dot in the appropriate cell of the chart if the work is in. If the cell is ✗'d, that work hasn't been done. Then once I've corrected the work, the dot becomes an OK. If the work was not okay, then the dot becomes a DO, which means "Do Over."

It's a rigorous approach, but it's an approach which unmistakably demonstrates your will forces, your intention for thoroughness. Having such a chart can inspire your unorganized, or lugubrious, or slothful types, while making your eager beavers feel recognized. When such a chart appears, nothing more need be said. You will see that students often congregate before it, out of interest, to make sure they're up to speed. Theoretically, such a public display might raise the question of shaming. But, actually, I've never experienced any student shamed. There's very little that the students don't already know about each other, and basically, they don't check the chart for anyone's progress but their own. The homework tracking chart objectifies the need to stay on track. At a glance, we all know where we are.

To correct the many exercises we do in class, I collect the students' binders once or twice during a main lesson block and designate misspelled words, punctuation mistakes, or grammar problems. I mark all mistakes, but I don't mark for grammar we have not yet learned. When I return the binders, I remind the students that ANY uncorrected mistakes found when I collect the binder at the end of the block will detract from overall achievement. (See the section on "Tracking and Evaluating.")

Spelling Corrections

Spelling mistakes get circled. I eschew red pens, they are so clichéd, preferring green or purple or turquoise—anything but red (and I expect the students to write using blue or black ink).

All (well, almost all) mistakes must be corrected. The misspelled word will be written out on the back of the original assignment (or on a new page if there is no space—with that new page stapled to the original) correctly three times (3W) or five times (5W) or ten times (10W). Depending on the student's level of proficiency, I decide which of these three levels to apply. If it just an honest, ordinary, regular mistake, then the norm is 3W. If I think that this student really knows better but didn't bother to check, then it will be a 5W. Or is this a recurring mistake for this student? Then a 10W is called for. What's more, these corrections have to be legible and neat. If a new mistake is now inadvertently replicated, then the new mistake has to be corrected twice as many times. And we, the teachers, have to keep track. Okay, perhaps not every time, but with enough spot checks to keep the students on their toes. And in the case of known escape artists, we have to up the ante with more focus.

A refinement of the Word correction is the Sentence correction, which would be indicated by 3S, 5S or—rarely—a 10S. If, for example, we've just worked on the *its/it's* pitfall, and I find it unapologetically staring at me, I would most likely call for the 5S correction. The students generally see the logic of having to correct a sentence when the word by itself is innocent. If the sentence is particularly long, I might show mercy by indicating, with square brackets, the part of the sentence to be corrected five times. I ask the student to underline the naughty knotty spot, but honestly, it's the rare student who follows through on that detail. Nevertheless, I remind them frequently.

A very effective method I've invented and used in spelling confusion extremes is the "spelling dictionary." This is not a published dictionary, but a notebook with a page for each letter of the alphabet, where the student keeps track of his or her own mistakes. If the student misspells *generus* [sic], for example, then in addition to the 3W correction on the original composition, the corrected word goes onto the G page, and the next time that word is misspelled, a little check mark is placed next to the word, and then we can see how often we make that mistake. This is a consciousness-raising device with a long reach. It is also inconvenient, a bother for student and teacher, but it is a wonderful device for getting students to pay attention. Needless to add, a spot check by the teacher is requisite. You have to painstakingly go over an assignment, check the first set of corrections, then check the student's spelling dictionary. But, again, you needn't do it every day. Perhaps there are particular students you want to check on after just a couple of assignments. Generally, though, collecting the original, the corrections, and the dictionary once in an unexpected while, works wonders.

No one wants to be a bad speller. Including me. English is my second language, and on the foundation of High German and Swiss German, I simply could not hear the difference between *pet* and *pat*. Of course that doesn't excuse my lifelong confusion of *-ible* with *-able* or *-ence* with *-ance*. "Uncorrected spelling is your fault," I admonish the students. "Catch me!" Overbearing as my spelling correction regime for youngsters may seem, I have found that they feel it's worth their while. What's more, more often than not, especially in boys, spelling ripens into an unexpectedly dependable skill around 10th grade. And that's without spell-check at hand.

Meanwhile, however, another way to manage the spelling scree is to divide the group into those who needn't show you their corrections before writing the final copy of their story and those who do need to get your approval first. This rewards the good spellers and motivates the challenged ones. It also means less supervision when the supervision is not really necessary.

Looking up words in a dictionary is a skill that should be learned by 5th grade. Like any skill, it requires practice. There's an inherent paradox in having to know how a word starts so as to find it in the dictionary. It takes some confidence, and only through practice can the confidence and skill be encouraged.

A really comprehensive dictionary—with synonyms, antonyms, examples and etymologies—is a great asset in any classroom. For the youngsters, a smaller paperback will do, but the teacher really needs to make a point of looking things up, or asking a student to do it. We have to demonstrate that there is no shame in looking up a word; on the contrary, it's necessary *research*.

I pay no attention to the inescapable "How do you spell…?" plea. In fact, I try to eradicate it. "Look it up!" is my response. I discourage neighbors from whispering correct spelling. "Best guess" practices are encouraged. During quizzes and tests that are not just about spelling, dictionaries on the desk are mandatory.

An unfair reality of the spelling snarl is that meticulous students, the ones who take the time to look up a word, are so careful and methodical that they run out of time during a test. In that case, I remind them (discreetly) that finishing the test trumps correct spelling. It's a time management issue and needs to be addressed obliquely, as the underlying reasons for this issue are usually deep-seated.

As already noted, poor spelling should not interfere with the teacher's appreciation of what the student is actually communicating.

Punctuation Corrections

Apart from spelling, punctuation provides us with the other potentially chaotic realm. My strategy for dealing with the missing question mark, the unnecessary comma, or the semicolons littering the page is similar to my approach to the spelling quagmire. I point out the mistake, and I want to see the correction. Whether the phrase or sentence in which the punctuation folly occurred has to be rewritten, and how often, depends on the gravity and frequency of the foolishness. In some cases, I'm satisfied if the final, or "clear," copy of the paper is correct. This means that the corrected draft has to be studied closely and compared painstakingly with the final copy. If you have a large class, you may provide yourself with the oxygen mask of spot checks.

Grammar Corrections

Grammar and syntax corrections often have to be provided by the teacher. In determining whether to show the student how to improve a phrase or sentence, I consider whether the student will understand my cryptic remarks or whether I really need to do the work for the student.

Other Corrections: Vocabulary, Syntax

One of my favorite correction devices is a squiggly line under a word, which means: Is this the best word here? I apply a variable scale: The best students have to figure out how to improve the word or phrase on their own.

Starting the Class with a Poem

For the first five years of my Waldorf career, I was a German teacher at the Rudolf Steiner School in New York City. I taught 5th through 11th grades. I had no formal Waldorf training. My extraordinary colleagues, many of whom had been my teachers when I'd attended the high school almost a decade earlier, and who constituted the Pantheon of Pioneer Waldorf Teachers in the US, provided me with so much more than training. From them I gained an ethos, profound pedagogical insights, and practiced practicalities. From my days as their pupil, I vividly remember the way so many of my classes had started with a poem. These were not mere tongue twisters or funny ditties. These were great poems by the likes of Shelley, Keats, Byron and others.

So I got into the habit of starting every German class I taught—5th through 11th grades—with a German poem. As a special subject teacher roaming from one class to the next, sometimes as many as five a day, I developed an ear for the students' participation in these recitations. I could hear the mood of the class and quickly spot the restless and distracted. Later, when I became a class teacher, I continued the habit. After the Morning Verse, we worked on poems.

Starting the creative writing block classes with poetry makes complete sense. In recent years, in 7th and 8th grades, we've worked on "Ozymandias," by Shelley, Shakespeare sonnets, excerpts from "The Prelude" and "The Daffodil" by Wordsworth, and poems by Keats, Byron, Frost, and others. I also start with poetry when teaching adults.

It's a wonderful way to "tune" the class. We don't take long, maybe five or six minutes, but we *work hard*. We don't drone, we don't mindlessly repeat the words. We think about what we're saying, we articulate, we project, we stand tall; our hands are not in our pockets, we breathe. And we learn great poetry by heart. Invariably, the block review, or final test, includes the optional possibility of writing the poem we learned. It's always rewarding to see how many students learned the poem by heart. I never count spelling or punctuation for these attempts.

"I remember starting with a poem at the beginning of main lesson," is the first sentence of another former 8th grader, now a junior in high school. This is a very capable student. She ends her remarks about the creative writing block with, "Unfortunately, I do not remember too many specifics." All the more notable, then, that she does remember starting with a poem.

Working with Adults

The method suggested by the various exercises and tasks presented here works equally well for adult students. What distinguishes them from their younger counterparts in high school or upper elementary school are the pace of instruction, and the degree of expectation. Faster and higher.

When I started working as an adult educator in Waldorf teacher training, I taught a course called "The History and Literature of the English Language." We covered a lot of ground, much of it focused on Rudolf Steiner's many references to the origin, the esoteric background and the essence of language. Little to no creative writing was involved in those early courses. By the time I retired 26 years later, that course had transmogrified into a writing course in which much of what we worked on was fundamentally the same as what I offered the younger students. For the adults, I included quotations from the works of the great romantic poets, quotations about the imagination. William Blake, William Wordsworth, Samuel Taylor Coleridge, Percy Bysshe Shelley, John Keats, Lord George Byron—all of them worked deliberately and long to hone the imagination. (see quotations by the Romantic poets on imaginations in Appendix)

Not for nothing did Owen Barfield call his book about anthroposophy *Romanticism Comes of Age*. The Romantics understood that the imagination leads to truth. For the adults I also included the American Transcendentalists, especially Thoreau and Emerson. Emerson, who described his writing by saying, "I am a rocket manufacturer." Emerson, who perfectly understood what Rudolf Steiner described as *Logos*:

> The Logos is the mediator between the world of sense and the unimaginable God. By steeping himself in cognition, man unites with the Logos. The Logos becomes embodied in him. The person who has developed spiritually is the vehicle of the Logos. Above the Logos is God, beneath is the perishable world. It is man's vocation to form the link between the two.[30]

Emerson unfurls the tenets of language as Logos somewhat differently, but unmistakably, in Chapter Four of his groundbreaking essay, "Nature":

1. Words are signs of natural facts.
2. Particular natural facts are symbols of particular spiritual facts.
3. Nature is the symbol of spirit.

These intellectual buttresses, making the case historically for imaginative writing which rests in truth, don't automatically improve a person's writing. Furthermore, just being a grownup does not a better writer make. On the contrary. As adults we want to stand our ground. We get defensive even more easily than the thin-skinned adolescent. We identify so strongly with our own words that we cannot bear to part with any of them, even if we have weighed our writing down with endless, innumerable, redundant adjectives. If we are "imagination poor," we feel stranded and dazed when asked to pretend that we are in a forest at dusk. What do we see? Let's close our eyes. What do we see? Terror grips us. We see nothing.

Currently I teach a small group of adult students in the setting of a continuing education course offered by the local high school district. Talk about a motley crew! No one has anything in common with anyone else. Yet they are all very grateful to be getting specific guidelines to improve their writing. They are beginning to understand that quite often less is more, that the pictures they are describing must be inherently logical, that to be reader-friendly is not weak. Our hour and a half session can easily deal with just one set of sentences, just one setting, most recently, the beach at dusk. I will let them speak for themselves:

> Writing pictorially has entirely demystified the writing process for me. Here is a clear path—not easy, but clear—through which I can work hard and, step by step, access the spiritual process of creative writing. For years I have asked myself: How can I draw the reader in and convey my emotional experience to them without being boring? Writing out of the picture was a revelation. Writing about the feelings falls flat, and writing with information doesn't convey the emotional experience. But writing out of the picture, giving the fine details that we ourselves notice without even realizing it, to form our own emotional reaction, draws the reader in irresistibly.
>
> For me, it was also heartwarming to be able to spend so much time just working, crossing out words, thinking about the picture, rewriting, noticing some more details, and then rewriting some more, as a process by which I can access the creative part of us that brings our stories forth.

The writer has a background in technology and science and a PhD. What she quickly realized is that she is apt to veer toward explanation and fact; only describing the scene was a challenge.

However, she was quick to grasp the method and began to enjoy the crossings out and arrows, the words she circled and underlined, the challenge of keeping herself in check.

Here is another:

> This no-nonsense approach to teaching creative writing stimulates my mind and enhances my creativity. She emphasizes the importance of description rather than information, of logical thinking and of smooth transitions. Dorit gives personalized, perceptive feedback on our writing samples which include setting and character development. Not only has my writing improved, but I also appreciate reading well-written novels more.

As I visit former students who are now teachers, I often hear about the value of having learned to write pictorially; it provided the confidence to teach pictorially. Here is a recent comment:

> The writing course helped me learn how to look more carefully at the world. I began to observe life in a different way and to see things from a more objective perspective. Through the exercises Dorit had us do, I came to see more clearly how to go about writing in a way that paints a picture for the reader—creating images with words.

Appendix
The Romantic Poets on Imagination

William Blake (1757–1827)
Vision of Imagination is a representative of what eternally exists, Really and Unchangeably.

Imagination is spiritual sensation.

May God us keep from single vision and Newton's sleep.

> *I rest not from my great task!*
> *To open the Eternal Worlds, to open the immortal Eyes*
> *Of Man inwards, into the Worlds of Thought, into Eternity*
> *Ever expanding in the Bosom of God, the Human Imagination.*

Singular and Particular Detail is the Foundation of the Sublime.

To Generalize is to be an Idiot. To Particularize is the Alone Distinction of Merit…

William Wordsworth (1770–1850)
Poetry should
> *…take incidents from common life*
> *…be composed in language really used by men*
> *…be colored by imagination*

Samuel Taylor Coleridge (1772–1834)

*The primary Imagination I hold to be the living power and prime
Agent of all human Perception, and as a repetition in the finite mind
of the eternal act of creation in the infinite I AM.*

Percy Bysshe Shelley (1792–1822)

*Reason is the enumeration of qualities already known; imagination
is the perception of the value of those qualities, both separately and
as a whole. Reason respects the differences, and imagination the
similitudes of things. Reason is to the imagination as the instrument
to the agent, as the body to the spirit, as the shadow to the substance.*

John Keats (1795–1821)

I want a brighter word than bright.

*I am certain of nothing but of the holiness of the Heart's affections
and the truth of the Imagination – Whatever the imagination seizes
as Beauty must be truth – whether it existed before or not … The
Imagination may be compared to Adam's dream – he awoke and
found it truth.*

Endnotes

1   Rudolf Steiner. *Man's Being, His Destiny and World Evolution*. Oslo, May 1923 (GA 226), trans. Erna McArthur.

2   "We should speak in ordinary language to the child and avoid the use of this baby-talk. At first the child will naturally only babble in imitation of words, but we ourselves must not copy this babbling. To use the babbling, imperfect speech of the child to him is to injure his digestive organs. Once more the spiritual becomes physical, and works directly into the bodily organs. And everything that we do spiritually for the child constitutes a physical training, for the child is not all individual. Many later defects in the digestive system are caused by a child's having learned to speak in a wrong way." Rudolf Steiner. *Education and Modern Spiritual Life* (Ilkley Course), Chapter III, August 10, 1923 (GA 307).

3   When teaching adults, a discussion of *Logos* would be appropriate.

4   Christine A. Lindberg, ed. *Oxford American Writer's Thesaurus*, Second Edition. New York: Oxford University Press, 2008.

5   Barry Lopez, ed. *Home Ground: Language for an American Landscape*. San Antonio, TX: Trinity University Press, 2006.

6   David Grambs and Ellen S. Levine. *The Describer's Dictionary: A Treasury of Terms & Literary Quotations for Readers and Writers*. New York: W.W. Norton and Company, 1993.

7   "Heaven's Gate," from *Dark Energy* by Robert Morgan, copyright ©2015 by Robert Morgan. Used by permission of Viking Books, an imprint of Penguin Publishing Group, a division of Penguin Random House, LLC.

8   Oddly, Edward Bulwer-Lytton, the author of these words, is hailed by Rudolf Steiner as a paragon of novel writing.

9   Viawit. (2013, March 18. "It was a dark and stormy night." Retrieved from https://pearlsofprofundity.wordpress.com/2013/03/18/it-was-a-dark-and-stormy-night/

10 The Phrase Finder. Retrieved from http://www.phrases.org.uk/meanings/it-was-a-dark-and-stormy-night.html

11 Dorit Winter. *The Art and Science of Teaching Composition*. Fair Oaks, CA: AWSNA Publications, 1998.

12 Rudolf Steiner. *Education for Adolescents*, lecture 4, June 15, 1921, Herndon, VA: SteinerBooks, 1996.

13 Imagination rich / imagination poor is one of the four polarities Rudolf Steiner alludes to in various pedagogical lectures and can be found in: *Education for Adolescents* (GA 302), lecture 4; *Developmental Insights - Discussions between Doctors and Teachers*, Chapter 2; *Constitutional Types in School-Age Children* by Michaela Glöckler, MD, Fair Oaks, CA: AWSNA Publications.

14 See the "basic" or "subsidiary" exercises in Rudolf Steiner. *Guidance in Esoteric Training*, Sussex, UK: Rudolf Steiner Press, 1994.

15 Essberger, Josef. "Passive Voice." The English Club. Retrieved from https://www.englishclub.com/grammar/verbs-voice-active-passive.htm

16 "Active Voice and Passive Voice." Retrieved from http://www.talkenglish.com/grammar/active-passive-voice.aspx

17 Merriam-Webster. "Words at Play: How to Use Lay and Lie." Retrieved from http://www.merriam-webster.com/words-at-play/how-to-use-lay-and-lie

18 Grammar Slammer. English Plus. Retrieved from http://englishplus.com/grammar/00000233.htm

19 Rudolf Steiner said of his colleague, Dr. Ita Wegman, that what distinguished her was her "courage to heal." "Polarities in Health,

Illness and Therapy," a lecture in Pennmenmawr, August 28, 1923 (GA 319). *Anthroposophische Menschenerkenntnis und Medizin*, Bibliogr.-Nr. 319, published by the Rudolf Steiner Nachlassverwaltung, Dornach, Switzerland, 1971.

20 www.cartoonstock.com, with permission.

21 NON SEQUITUR © 2012 Wiley Ink, Inc. Dist. by ANDREWS MCMEEL SYNDICATION. Reprinted with permission. All rights reserved.

22 Zijderveld, Anton C. "On Clichés." Literary Devices. Retrieved from http://literarydevices.net/cliche/

23 "Impression," by Dorit Winter, anthologized in *The Key*, the literary magazine of the Rudolf Steiner High School, New York City, 1963-64.

24 "Examples of Personification." Retrieved from http://examples.yourdictionary.com/examples-of-personification.html

25 Rudolf Steiner, *Faculty Meetings with the Teachers of the Free Waldorf School Stuttgart*, faculty meeting on February 6, 1923. Private publication for teachers. Also in *Menschenerkenntnis und Unterrichtsgestaltung* [Knowledge of Man and the Form of the Lesson], Bibliography No 302, 1978, Lecture on June 13, 1921.

26 Konnikova, Maria. "What's Lost as Handwriting Fades." *The New York Times*, Science. (2014, June 2). Retrieved from http://www.nytimes.com/2014/06/03/science/whats-lost-as-handwriting-fades.html

27 Valerio, Pablo. (2011, December 6). "The Importance of Cursive Writing." Retrieved from http://www.enterpriseefficiency.com/author.asp?section_id=1077&doc_id=236382

28 Spear-Swerling, Louise. "The Importance of Teaching Handwriting. (2006). Reading Rockets, WETA Public Broadcasting. Retrieved from http://www.readingrockets.org/article/importance-teaching-handwriting

29 Steinmetz, Katy. "Five Reasons Kids Should Still Learn Cursive
    Writing." (2014, June 4). Time. Retrieved from http://time.com/
    2820780/five-reasons-kids-should-still-learn-cursive-writing/

    and

    Asherson, Suzanne Baruch. "The Benefits of Cursive Go Beyond
    Writing." (2013, April 30). *The New York Times*, Opinion Page.
    Retrieved from http://www.nytimes.com/roomfordebate/2013/
    04/30/should-schools-require-children-to-learn-cursive/
    the-benefits-of-cursive-go-beyond-writing

30 Rudolf Steiner. *Christianity as a Mystical Fact: And the Mysteries
    of Antiquity*, chapter 12, trans. Andrew Welburn, Herndon, VA:
    SteinerBooks, 1997.

Acknowledgments

My heartfelt thanks to all the students who,
over the past four decades,
took up the challenge to *Write On!*

About the Author

Dorit Winter, MA, brings a cosmopolitan background to all her undertakings. Born in Jerusalem in 1947, she attended kindergarten in Zürich, primary school in Johannesburg and Cape Town, and junior and senior high schools in New York City, graduating from the Rudolf Steiner High School in 1964.

Dorit began her Waldorf career in 1973 as a German and class teacher at the Rudolf Steiner School in New York City. Seven years later, she joined the Great Barrington Rudolf Steiner School, where she coordinated the founding of a new high school. In 1989 she became founder and director of Rudolf Steiner College's satellite teacher training program in San Francisco. In 2001 she accepted the directorship of Bay Area Center for Waldorf Teacher Training, from which she retired in 2014.

A former member of the Hague Circle/International Forum of Waldorf/Steiner Schools, Dorit continues to travel nationally and internationally to lecture, give workshops, and teach. A full listing of her Waldorf activities can be found at www.doritwinterwaldorf.com.

Dorit's work as a painter influenced her pictorial approach to writing. Her paintings can be viewed at www.doritwinter.com.

Made in United States
North Haven, CT
23 February 2023

33061150R00113